# Scarves &

## Wraps

25 gorgeous designs
inspired by nature

Jill Denton

D&C
David and Charles

*This book is dedicated to my wonderful Mum, who introduced me to the amazing world of textiles and stitch, and who would have been very happy and proud to know that her daughter had made it her career and had written a book celebrating it.*

A DAVID & CHARLES BOOK

David & Charles is an F&W Publications Inc. company
4700 East Galbraith Road
Cincinnati, OH 45236

First UK edition published 2008-06-11

Conceived and produced by Breslich & Foss Ltd
2A Union Court
20-22 Union Road
London SW4 6JP

Photography and styling by **Lizzie Orme**
Commissioned by **Janet Ravenscroft**
Design by **Lisa Tai**

ISBN-13:978-0-7153-3003-6
ISBN-10:0-7153-3003-6

Printed in China for David & Charles, Brunel House, Newton Abbot, Devon

Visit our website at www.davidandcharles.co.uk

David & Charles books are available from all good bookshops; alternatively you can contact our Orderline on 0870 9908222 or write to us at FREEPOST EX2 110, D&C Direct, Newton Abbot, TQ12 4ZZ (no stamp required UK only)

10 9 8 7 6 5 4 3 2 1

# contents

# introduction

I can't remember a time when I didn't sew or make things. My mother taught me basic stitches almost as soon as I could safely hold a needle, and she was always there to help, encourage and sort me out when something went wrong. My first attempts at school were not particularly impressive: I can remember having to stitch a tiny hemstitch all around a red gingham apron when I was about six, which at the time seemed like a mammoth task that took weeks to complete, and I still have the handkerchief case upon which I clumsily embroidered flowers in lazy daisy stitch. (Lazy daisy is still one of my favourite stitches!) Then there was my first project at boarding school – a nightdress made out of brushed nylon; even that disaster didn't kill my enthusiasm for sewing. I stitched and knitted my way through my twenties and thirties, picking up and discarding many other crafts along the way. But although I enjoyed learning all these other techniques, my passion has always been for stitching and creating beautiful surfaces, garments and objects. I first discovered the fascination of making handmade felt many years ago, while studying on a foundation course in Art and Design at college. More experimentation with felt continued during a degree course in fashion and textiles, after which I used it more and more in my work, until ultimately I was hooked! Feltmaking is addictive and can become an obsession, so beware those of you who are still felt virgins. After you have tried it once,

Having learnt the basic techniques, each maker will develop his or her preferred, and probably unique, techniques. The more experienced the maker, the more unusual the techniques and equipment used may seem to the uninitiated. People who know nothing about feltmaking may wonder why feltmakers have washing lines full of towels, sheets of bubble wrap and plastic bags or why they can be seen in a local home-improvement store checking out the best-value swimming-pool liner or electric sander. I hope that, by the end of this book, you will understand some of the idiosyncrasies of feltmaking and that some of the mysteries and secrets will have been revealed.

there's often no looking back.Now, years later, I find myself recognised as a successful felt artist and tutor and – a real honour – invited to write a book about it.

Felt is one of the oldest textiles known to man. It is an unusual method of fabric construction in that, although all feltmakers do the same thing – laying out the wool, wetting, soaping and manipulating the fibres to make them shrink – no two feltmakers make it in exactly the same way. There is no right or wrong way. Some feltmakers use bubble wrap, some cane blinds, some fabric; some use liquid soap, others use a bar of soap.

## My inspiration

My work is all about colour and texture. I draw my inspiration from everything around me and carry a sketchbook and a camera with me at all times to record the things that I see. I then use wool fibres in the same way that a painter uses paint to translate my ideas and thoughts into images. I love the slight unpredictability of felt and the way the colours stay pure and hold their vibrancy throughout the process. Nothing is ever wasted. Occasionally when something goes wrong, I re-work it and change it into something else, so that a mistake becomes a happy accident. That is the beauty of felt: it's very forgiving and so versatile that even disasters can be transformed into something practical or beautiful.

All the scarves and wraps in this book are inspired by things that I have seen and are, in a way, a development of my artwork. For me, nothing is more beautiful than nature. Wherever possible I have included an image of my inspiration so that you can see where my ideas come from. I hope that this will inspire you not only to try to make some of the projects yourself, but also to create your own designs.

Step-by-step instructions are given for eleven of the scarves and wraps in this book and briefer instructions for the other fourteen, but it's important to understand that feltmaking is a unique process and that a felt design can never be re-created exactly. It's also impossible to guarantee precise results from any instructions as, even when they are following the same step-by-step instructions, no two people will produce an identical piece. The end result depends on several factors: the fibres you use, how thickly you lay out the fibres, how much you rub the pre-felt, how hard you roll. Even the weather conditions can affect the process, as felt will form more quickly if the weather is warm and damp than if it is cold and dry. Most of the measurements that are given are approximate as, due to the nature of the materials, it is not possible to predict the exact size of the finished piece.

Many feltmakers always use hot water as part of their process, but I have chosen to make these scarves mostly with cold water. Hot water is used for some of the scarves, usually towards the end to speed up the shrinking process. The projects are graded according to difficulty:

✿       easy projects for the novice

✿✿      more difficult pieces

✿✿✿    the most challenging designs

The Summer Flowers scarf on (pages 22–25) will get you started on basic feltmaking. It is important to master the basic techniques of feltmaking and get a good feel for the fibre before you move on to more advanced techniques. If you try to move on too fast, you may well end up with a disaster on your hands and feel disappointed and frustrated. So take it easy, experiment and practise with the simpler scarves – then move on to the more difficult ones.

# materials

In this section, I'm going to explain what I use to make my felt. Feltmaking is a very personal process and you will undoubtedly discover your own favourite materials and techniques – but if you're a complete novice, it helps to know what works for other people.

## Choosing wool and embellishments

Most of my scarves and artwork are made from 100 per cent merino wool tops or fleece. Merino is easy to felt and is good for making both very fine and thick felt. Blue-faced Leicester is another very easy wool to felt and was used for the Woodland Wrap (page 98). It has an attractive curl to it, which adds a little texture. The Sycamore scarf (page 66) is made from Shetland wool and the Treebark scarf (page 96) from Black Welsh. Both these fibres felt well, but have a coarser feel and look to them, and produce a light and lofty felt. Any animal hair can be felted, so it's worth experimenting with different types to discover their qualities and the effects they produce.

To add interest and texture, I often include a variety of other fibres to the surface of the scarves. Wensleydale curls are wonderful and I've used them in three scarves in this book, the Moorland scarf (page 78), the Forest Green scarf (page 90) and the Woodland wrap (page 98). I often pull off one or two curls and mix them in with the merino. Wensleydale fleece is available in fabulous colours and stays quite shiny throughout the felting process. Mohair fibres are a little shorter but lustrous and also work well. Tussah silk, which is available in many colours, white and off-white, creates a lovely sheen when added to the top layer of fleece, either mixed in with the wool fibres or laid on top. There are many other wonderful fibres available from feltmaking suppliers for the crafts person to experiment with.

*Above: Dyed wool tops ready for felting. Ready-dyed tops are available in hundreds of gorgeous shades, although you can buy undyed fleece and dye it yourself.*

I also have a huge box of knitting yarns that I have collected over the years that I frequently dip into. (Never throw anything away if you're going to make felt; you never know when you may need it!) Fancy yarns, slubbed yarns, mohair and chenille are particularly useful. As a general rule, the higher the percentage of natural fibres, the better the yarn will adhere to the felt, but manmade yarns can also be

*Above: A selection of threads and yarns that I often incorporate into my feltmaking: fancy knitting yarns in various thicknesses, in both manmade and natural fibres, embroidery threads, rayon and silk threads, mohair and Wensleydale curls.*

used with a little bit of persuasion. Embroidery threads, recycled sari silk, sewing threads, scraps of fabric, lace, ribbon, buttons, beads: the list of things that can be worked into or used to decorate felt is extensive.

For making nuno felt, where the wool fibres are felted onto a loosely woven fabric, I prefer to use silk – chiffon, georgette, organza or tulle. However, you can felt onto any loosely woven fabric and I also use viscose or cotton muslin as a base. Some of my best finds have been in charity shops, which can be a valuable source of vintage fabrics, buttons and other useful things. Charity shops are also a good place to find old books with beautiful images, photographs and illustrations, which can be wonderful sources of inspiration for textile designs.

# equipment

One of the great things about feltmaking is that you don't need any fancy or expensive equipment. You will probably already have most of what you need at home. The essentials are:

- Old towels
- Bubble wrap
- Thin plastic sheeting
- Soap (I use olive oil soap, which is kind to the hands and is preferred by most feltmakers as it works well with wool)
- Rubber or surgeon's gloves if you have sensitive skin
- Plastic bags
- An old plastic bottle for sprinkling water (a milk bottle with holes punched in the lid is perfect)
- Water spray for very fine work (a plant sprayer or an old kitchen spray bottle will do)
- Washing-up bowl
- Cane blind and small cane mat
- Swimming 'noodle', length of pipe insulation, broom handle or similar (I prefer to use a noodle; when it's tied up, rolled in the middle of a cane blind, it grips well and doesn't slip)
- Fabric ties (I use old T-shirts cut into strips 2.5cm/1 in. wide, as the fabric has enough 'give' to make a nice, firm knot)
- Scissors
- Sewing kit
- Black marker pen

*Opposite: Basic feltmaking equipment. Any items that you do not already have at home, such as cane blinds or swimming noodles, can be purchased from local stores at very little cost.*

## finishing and care of your scarves

Although the instructions for making the scarves vary somewhat, the finishing process is the same for all of them. When you have finished the shrinking/felting process, rinse your scarf in cold water several times until all traces of soap have disappeared. Then give the scarf one final rinse in a bowl of water to which you have added a few drops of vinegar. This is to neutralise any traces of alkali that may remain from the soap. Gently squeeze out as much water as possible, then reshape the scarf and dry it flat. If you wish to press the scarf, press it on the back, using an iron on the wool setting, while the scarf is still slightly damp.

To clean your scarf, gently hand wash it in cool water using a liquid soap designed for handwashing woollens. Rinse the scarf in cold water and dry it as described above. If you care for your scarf properly it will last a very long time. But do watch out for moths — felt's worst enemy!

# inspiration for textile designs

For me, the inspiration and the design process are as important as the finished product. Not having had any formal art training when I was younger, I had trouble for years processing my ideas. I used to look around me and see so many wonderful things, but I just didn't know how to turn my ideas into projects, which was extremely frustrating. Then I went to college. Probably the most valuable thing that I learnt there was how to open my eyes and really 'see'. Here are a few simple tips on how to translate your ideas and inspirations into designs.

First, always carry a camera and a sketchbook with you. There's nothing worse than seeing something amazing and not having anything to record it with or on. Many people are scared of drawing and they think they can't do it. If you are one of these people, don't worry: take a photo and stick it in your sketchbook later – but make sure that, at the time, you write down brief notes about what you see. What colours and textures can you see? What time of day is it and what is the weather like? (Both these factors can affect the colours.) What sounds can you hear? Can you smell anything? All these things will help you re-create the image in your mind when you are back at home. Collect pictures, illustrations and photographs of things that interest you, for whatever reason, and keep them in an image bank; a stationery folder with plastic sleeves will do perfectly.

Look at an object very carefully. Say you're inspired by a leaf, for example. Hold it in your hand and feel it. Smell it. Listen to it. Explore it with all your senses and keep your mind open. Examine the colours. Concentrate on the shape and the details, such as where the lines on the leaf lead. Look at the texture, the shape of the edges and the veins.

If you are looking at a flower, look at the shapes of the petals. How many petals are there? How are they attached to the centre of the flower and to the stem?

*Right: Inspiration can be found anywhere: look out for lichens and rock plants, such as these growing on top of an old stone wall.*

*Above:* In this scene of a woodland in spring, the intense blue of the carpet of bluebells contrasts with the fresh greens of the foliage. You could use both the colours and the shapes in a scene such as this for inspiration.

Look at the stamens. Although a flower is a complex structure, try to break it down into simple shapes that can later be reproduced in felt.

Then, if you feel confident enough, draw your object in your sketchbook or on a piece of paper. A simple line drawing will allow you to concentrate on developing your composition and will help your brain to focus on the shape and form of your object. Don't worry that your sketch isn't perfect: it's for your reference and no one else's. If you really feel you can't draw, then don't worry – just trace the image from a photo or a magazine. If the image is too small, enlarge it on a photocopier. You can also use a photocopier to play with scale: interesting shapes and patterns appear when you enlarge images. Or simply draw around the object, using it as a template.

## Be selective

When you find a subject that appeals to you, there's often a temptation to include too many different elements without focusing on what it is that's really important. Use a viewfinder – a piece of card with a shape cut out of it – to help you be more selective. Make your own viewfinder by cutting a small square (4cm/1.5 in.) in the centre of a 10 x 15cm (4 x 6in.) piece of card. Find a photo or an illustration that appeals to you, place the viewfinder over it and move it around until you have found an interesting composition.

I use exactly the same process for developing my ideas, whether they come from seascapes, landscapes or a simple object. At this stage, I decide what colours I am going to use for the background and for the design part. Sometimes I may use as many as 30 or more different shades in a piece of work, but I would advise a beginner to start with a more modest palette of maybe four to six colours or shades; then, as you become more confident with the technique, you can be more adventurous with colour.

The number of colours also depends, of course, on the object you are using. For example, the Pebble

Stripes scarf on page 60 was inspired by pebbles from a beach in Cornwall. I studied these pebbles carefully and extracted just four delicate colours – buttermilk, grey, soft brown and sage green – to use in my felt design.

A more complicated example is the Sycamore scarf on page 66. A photograph of autumn leaves was

**Above:** *The pebbles that inspired the Pebble Stripes scarf on page 60 have an amazing variety of colours and shades.*

**Left:** *The delicate hues of bougainvillaea petals are enhanced by the clear blue sky. The strong lines of the white roof provide a strong contrast.*

*Left: These frost-encrusted leaves have deep, rich colours and fascinating shapes.*

*Below left: The twisted, sun-bleached limbs of a hurricane-damaged tree and the pure white sand contrast sharply with the deep azure ocean.*

*Below right: The interior of a conch shell, weatherbeaten and worn smooth, is a perfect spiral – an intriguing shape to use as the basis for a textile design.*

my inspiration and from this I chose a plain warm brown as the background, with vibrant shades of red, yellow, rust and burgundy for the leaves.

I have included templates for the designs in this book on pages 124–127, but when you find a subject that appeals, you can easily make your own templates by drawing around objects or tracing photos.

When you have positioned the motifs on your scarf, stand back and make sure that the design is well balanced. Imagine the scarf draped around your neck and work out where the design will fall. Have fun playing around and finding what works for you. The more fun you have designing and making your scarf, the more successful it will be.

# country garden

Summer is the time to relax with a book and a long, cool drink and to enjoy the profusion of colour that the garden offers. In this chapter, you will find instructions for making light, delicate scarves and throws that are just perfect for long summer evenings. The designs are inspired by flowers of every colour and shade. Daisies are a particular favourite of mine and often appear in my work; the magnificent shasta daisies were the inspiration for the scarf shown opposite and described on page 38. Traditional cottage gardens and wildflower meadows (so pretty and so delicate) also fuel my design ideas.

# summer flowers

**Summer flowers** was inspired by the blossoms, scents and colours of old-fashioned cottage gardens. Plant names such as hollyhock, lavender, delphinium, aquilegia, foxglove and lupin all conjure up images of a profusion of colour and texture. The delicate pinks and mauves of this scarf were chosen to bring to mind these summer varieties.

The flower and leaf motifs are created by cutting shapes from silk fabric and felting them onto the background. I used silk georgette for the flowers, but any fine, loosely woven fabric will do, provided it is made from natural fibres. The motifs can be outlined with machine or hand stitches to add extra definition, or decorated with beads.

You can make the scarf gossamer thin, by using only 25g (¾ oz) of fleece, or slightly thicker and more substantial by using 50g (2 oz), as I did in this example. You can either handcard or mix the colours yourself or buy them ready carded and mixed. The latter approach saves a lot of time and effort – especially if you are a novice feltmaker!

degree of difficulty
✿

tools and materials

towel

2 sheets of bubble wrap, 40 x 165cm (16 x 65 in.)

25 or 50g (¾ or 2 oz) merino wool tops in mixed pinks, mauve and purple

flower template on page 124

scraps of loosely woven fabric for flower and leaf design

fabric scissors

net, 40 x 165cm (16 x 65 in.)

plastic bottle with holes in lid

olive oil soap

small plastic bag

swimming 'noodle' or similar and ties

finished size

20 x 135cm (8 x 53 in.)

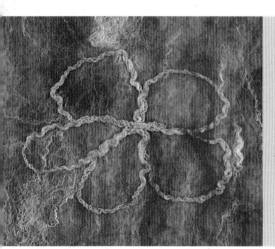

## variation

Instead of a solid shape cut from silk, such as the flowers used in the main project, you can achieve delicate outlines by laying down lengths of knitting yarn. Over the years I've gathered a collection of interesting yarns that I frequently use in my feltmaking. If you are using pure wool yarn (mohair, for example), lay the yarn on top of the laid-out fibres. If you are using yarn with a manmade content, 'veil' the yarn as you would the silk shapes in Step 5 on page 23.

# to make the summer flowers scarf

## tip

If you are a novice feltmaker, you may find it helpful to mark out the area of your scarf on the wrong side of the bubble wrap with a marker pen and a ruler before you begin. The lines will act as a guide as you lay out the fibres.

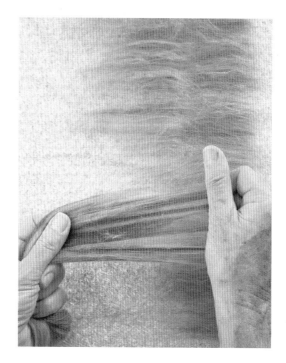

**1** Lay a towel on your work surface with a piece of bubble wrap, bubble side up, on top. Pull off and lay down a thin, even layer of merino fibres from the wool tops to cover the area of the scarf, laying all the fibres in one direction. Remember that the fibres will shrink during the felting process, so lay out fibres covering an area 25–30 per cent bigger than you want the finished scarf to be.

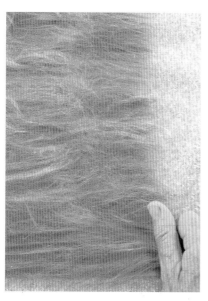

**2** Lay a few more fibres on each corner. This will strengthen the corners and give the scarf a neat, square finish.

**3** Lay out a second layer of fibres, placing them at right angles to the first layer. Lay extra fibres on each corner, making sure there is an even, slightly thicker layer along all the edges. This will ensure that all the edges and corners are firm.

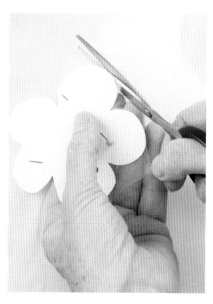

**4** Following the templates and using the fabric scissors, cut out approximately eight flower and ten leaf shapes from the silk fabric.

**5** Arrange the silk flowers and leaves on the fibres. 'Veil' the flowers and leaves with tiny wisps of fleece, which will hold them in place while felting. Place the flower and leaf motifs evenly along the scarf, but not too near the edge or they may become a little distorted during the rolling process.

**6** Cover the fibres with the net. Starting in the centre and working outwards, gradually and gently sprinkle the fibres all over with water. Press down gently on the surface with the flat of your hand to help the water soak into the wool fibres.

**7** Working from left to right, spread olive oil soap over the net. Keep your left hand firmly on the net while soaping, so as not to disturb the position of the wool fibres and silk motifs underneath. Soap helps the wool fibres absorb the water and assists the felting process.

**8** With your hand inside a plastic bag, gently rub the surface of the scarf in a circular motion using the flat of your hand, working your way from one end of the scarf to the other. This encourages the wool fibres to knit together. (The bag is to provide a larger, smoother flat surface area for rubbing, not to protect your hands.) Keep adding more water until the wool fibres are wet through. Continue rubbing for a couple of minutes, paying particular attention to the areas where you have placed the silk leaves or flowers.

▷

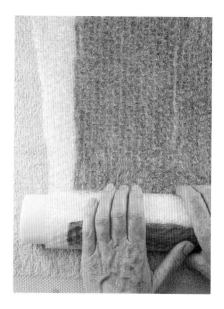

**9** Starting at one corner, gently peel back the net and check that the fibres are adhering to each other. If they are not holding together, replace the net and continue rubbing with a bagged hand until ready. When the fibres have adhered well, carefully remove the net completely.

**10** Fold over the bubble wrap along the edges of the scarf, just enough to get a straight edge, and press down to straighten and tidy up the edges. Unfold the bubble wrap.

**11** Place another sheet of bubble wrap over the scarf, bubble side down. With the scarf safely sandwiched between, firmly roll both layers around a cut-down swimming noodle or similar.

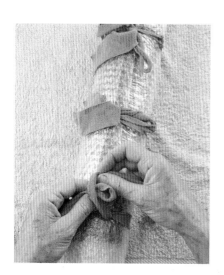

## tip

If you have a problem with your back or if your arms get tired, place the roll on the floor and use your feet to roll it backwards and forwards!

**12** Tie firmly around the swimming noodle using cord, string or strips of fabric cut from an old T-shirt. The T-shirt fabric has enough 'give' to make a nice, firm knot.

**13** Roll the swimming noodle backwards and forwards 100 times. Unroll the scarf, pull the scarf to shape and roll it up again, this time from the other end.

Roll 100 times more. Repeat twice more until the scarf has been rolled 600 times.

**14** Unwrap the bubble wrap sandwich and gently pull the scarf into shape.

**15** Fold the scarf up into a parcel, folding the edges inside, so that they meet in the middle. Drop the folded scarf on to your work surface from a height of 45–60cm (18–24 in.). Repeat 25 times. Open up the scarf and re-fold it, otherwise the fibres will felt along the folds and you will not be able to un-felt it. Drop it onto your work surface another 25 times. Repeat twice more. By this time the scarf should be reasonably well felted. If you want it to be more tightly felted, rinse it in hand-hot water and repeat this step twice more or until you are happy with the result.

**16** Rinse the finished scarf several times in cold water to remove any trace of soap, adding a few drops of vinegar to the final rinse. Pull the scarf into shape and let it dry flat. While the scarf is still slightly damp, iron it on the reverse, with the iron on a wool setting to smooth out any imperfections.

## tip

If you are using dark wool fibres for your scarf, use a light-coloured towel under the bubble wrap; if you are using light-coloured wool fibres, choose a dark towel. This makes it easier to get an even layer of wool, as you can see if there are any thin bits or gaps.

# pink lattice

**This scarf** was inspired by the gorgeous pink flowers with the crazy petals in the photo below. A final touch was added by felting a couple of flowers separately and stitching them to the completed scarf (see page 30). I added yellow centres to the flowers for contrast and an extra flash of colour. This scarf was made with fine strands, so it is very lightweight, but you can vary the look and feel by making the strands thicker and closer together. Another variation is to lay the fibres out on a piece of loosely woven fabric, so that the fibres adhere to the fabric. When the fibres shrink, the fabric puckers and produces a ruched, textured effect.

tools and materials

towel

2 sheets of bubble wrap, 40 x 140cm (16 x 55 in.)

50g (2 oz) pink merino wool tops

scraps of yellow merino wool tops and tussah silk for flowers

net, 40 x 140cm (16 x 55 in.)

plastic bottle with holes in lid

olive oil soap

small plastic bag

swimming 'noodle' or similar and ties

flower template on page 124

fabric scissors

sewing kit

finished size

20 x 110cm (8 x 43 in.)

# to make the pink lattice scarf

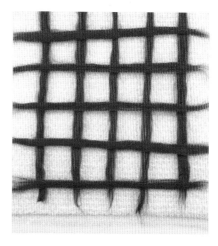

**1** Lay a towel on your work surface with a piece of bubble wrap, bubble side down, on top. Break off a length of pink merino wool tops the length you want the scarf to be, plus about 25 per cent extra to allow for shrinkage. Split this lengthwise into five even strands.

**2** Lay the strands on the bubble wrap, leaving a 5cm (2 in.) gap between each strand.

**3** Break off several lengths of pink merino wool top about 30cm (12 in.) long. Split each length into five strands, then lay each strand horizontally across the long strands, again with a 5cm (2 in.) gap between each strand, to form a grid.

**4** Cover the fibres with the net. Starting in the centre and working outwards, gradually and gently sprinkle the fibres with cold water. Press down gently on the surface with the flat of your hand to help the water soak into the wool fibres.

**5** Spread the olive oil soap over the net, being careful not to move the fibres underneath.

**6** With your hand inside a plastic bag, gently rub the fibres with your fingertips in a circular motion, working from one end of the scarf to the other.

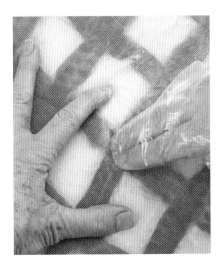

**7** Pay particular attention to the points where the fibres overlap, ensuring these fibres adhere well. Otherwise the scarf won't hold together.

**8** Peel back the net and check that the fibres are holding together. If they are not, replace the net and continue rubbing. When the fibres have adhered well, remove the net. At this stage, you may need to coax the fibres back tidily if they have spread out a little.

**9** Put another sheet of bubble wrap over the scarf, bubble side up. Roll both layers, with the scarf sandwiched in between, around a cut-down piece of swimming noodle or similar.

**10** Tie up the swimming noodle firmly. Roll the swimming noodle backwards and forwards 50 times. Unroll, pull the scarf into shape, roll up from the other end, tie and roll another 50 times. Repeat until you have rolled the scarf 400 times. Unwrap again, pull the scarf into shape and make sure that all the cross points have felted together. Remove the scarf from the bubble wrap, place it in a bowl of warm water and gently swish it around, squeezing and gently rubbing it in your hands to shrink and felt it a little more. Rinse several times in cold water until all traces of soap have been removed, adding a few drops of vinegar to the final rinse. Pull the scarf into shape and dry flat. Iron if required, using an iron on a wool setting.

## tip

If the cross points have not felted together sufficiently, repeat the rolling process in Step 9 until they have.

# to make the pink felt flowers

These pretty flowers are made from a separate piece of felt known as pre-felt, which is created when the fibres have been wetted, soaped and rubbed until they hold together. At this stage, as the felting process has not yet started, fibres can still be added or removed; pre-felt can be cut, stitched into, dried and re-wetted. It is at this stage that the template is used to cut out the motifs, which are then rolled to complete the felting process.

**1** Lay out a layer of fleece on a small piece of bubble wrap to cover an area about 6 in. (15cm) square.

**5** Blot with a towel to remove the excess water, then remove the net.

**2** Place another layer of fleece on top, at 90 degrees to the first layer.

**3** On top of this, place some yellow fibres in a circle to form the centre of the flower. I also added some tussah silk fibres to give the surface a shine.

**4** Cover with a small piece of net. Wet and soap the fleece. Rub gently until the fibres hold together. If you lift the net and rub the fibres with your fingertip, they should stay put. If they move, replace the net and rub again.

**6** Centre the template over one of the yellow circles, pin it onto the piece of pre-felt and cut out the required number of flowers.

**7** Place the flower shapes on a small piece of bubble wrap and proceed as in step 10 of the lattice scarf, on page 29. You will probably only have to roll the flowers about 100 times in total, as the felt is very fine.

**8** When all the fibres are lightly felted together, rinse the flowers in cold water and dry flat. Trim the edges if necessary, then stitch the flowers onto the scarf where required. I stitched them on with a few French knots for decorative effect.

# daisy brooch

**This brooch** was inspired by the daisy – so called because it is the 'day's eye', the first flower to open in the morning sunlight – although you could change the look completely by varying the shape of the flower. It can be used as a colourful accessory to brighten up any outfit. Decorative embroidery, both by hand and machine, adds a lovely finishing touch; you could further embellish the flower centre by stitching on a scattering of seed beads. Pins are readily available from most craft shops and are simple to stitch onto the back of felt brooches.

degree of difficulty
❀

tools and materials

towel

1 sheet of bubble wrap, 20 x 40cm (8 x 16 in.)

10g (½ oz) each of white and yellow merino wool tops

net, 20cm (8 in.) square

plastic bottle with holes in lid

olive oil soap

small plastic bag

template on page 124

brooch pin

fabric scissors

sewing kit

finished size

10cm (4 in.) in diameter

# to make the daisy brooch

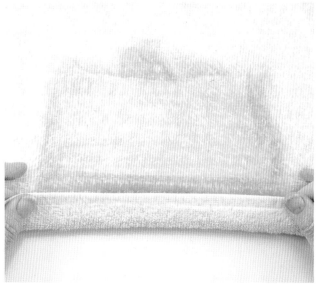

**1** Place the towel on your work surface, with the bubble wrap on top (either side up). At one end of the piece of bubble wrap, lay down two fairly thick layers of white merino fleece to cover an area about 15cm (6 in.) square, with the fibres of the second layer at right angles to the first. Lay down a third layer of yellow fleece at right angles to the middle layer.

**2** Lay a piece of net over the fibres. Wet, soap and rub the fibres with your hand until the fibres hold together. Remove the net, then fold over the rest of the bubble wrap to cover the fibres. As this is a very small piece of felt, you can roll it up in the bubble wrap and towel only. Roll 50 times, unroll, reshape, turn the piece 90 degrees, then roll up and roll another 50 times. Repeat until you have rolled 200 times, 50 in each direction.

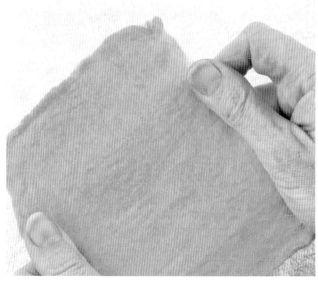

**3** Gently rub and manipulate the piece in your hand until it has shrunk to about 10cm (4 in.) square. Pull it into shape.

**4** Rinse the piece in cold water, wring out as much water as possible, reshape and flatten.

**5** Make the template out of paper or thin plastic, pin it onto the felt and cut it out using the fabric scissors.

**6** When the flower is dry, decorate the flower with machine stitching, by topstitching around the edge and stitching a spiral in the centre. Hand embroider a few French knots in the centre.

**7** Hand stitch a brooch pin to the back.

## tip

Why not make a bigger piece of felt and cut out several flowers? You can then stitch the flowers onto an old bag or garment to brighten it up and give it a new lease on life.

# wildflower meadow

**This wrap** is made from nuno felt – a technique in which felt and fabric are combined to produce a strong, but usually fine, fabric that drapes well. A fine layer of fleece is placed on the surface of the chosen fabric, usually a loosely woven, lightweight fabric of natural fibres and the wool fibres are then encouraged to penetrate the fabric, prior to felting. As the felting progresses, the fibres draw up the fabric to create a ruched effect.

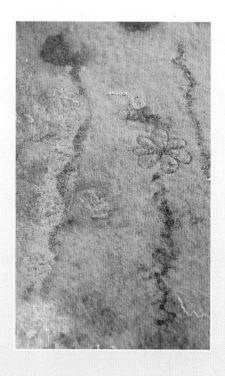

This project was inspired by the delicate flowers that grow wild in meadows in early summer – daisies, cornflowers, poppies and pretty grasses. For the fabric, I used a vintage floral silk scarf, probably from the 1950s or '60s. The decoration is a mixture of threads, yarns, silks, scraps of fabric, ribbon and lace, embellished after felting with the odd stitch here and there.

## Method of felting

First, I placed a towel and bubble wrap on my work surface. As the headscarf that I was using for the back of the wrap was square, I cut it

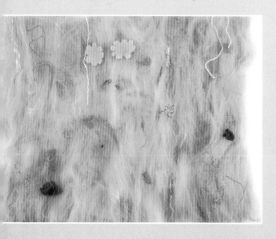

in half and placed it on the bubble wrap, overlapping the short edges in the middle to make one length.

Using a mix of different shades of green, I pulled off the wool fibres and laid them down in random directions on the silk. When the silk was completely covered in a thick, even layer of fibres, I decorated the wrap by laying down bits of yarn, silk fibres, scraps of fabric, ribbon, embroidery threads and sewing threads all over the green background, creating an exciting and well-balanced design.

The next stage was to make white and yellow pre-felts (see page 30).

I cut small flower shapes from them and placed them on the fibres.

I placed a piece of net over the wrap and soaped and rubbed it until all the decorative fibres and pre-felt motifs adhered firmly to the green background. I then removed the net, flipped the wrap over on the bubble wrap and rubbed the back gently all over to encourage the fibres to migrate through to the other side of the silk fabric. It's vital that this stage is complete before you move on to rolling the felt.

The final stage was to roll and rinse the wrap in the same way as the Summer Flowers scarf on page 20.

# green daisies

**Of all the summer flowers**, one of my favourites is the daisy. I love its simplicity and often can't resist sneaking a little one into a piece of work where perhaps it doesn't really belong. This design, set against a beautiful textured green background, was inspired by an amazing bed of shasta daisies.

## Method of felting

First, I laid out two layers of green fibres, as in the Summer Flowers scarf on page 20. Over the top layer, I placed a random selection of green threads, silks, yarns and scraps of fabric.

I placed a piece of net on top and then wetted, soaped and rubbed until the fibres just held together to form a pre-felt (see page 30). I then prepared two smaller pieces of pre-felt – one in white measuring 25cm (10 in.) square and one in yellow measuring 15cm (6 in.) square. From the white piece, I cut several strips 7–8mm (⅜ in.) wide, which I then cut down further into pieces about 5–6cm (2¼ in.) long for the daisy petals.

I worked out how many daisies I wanted in the design and then cut this number of circles 3cm (1½ in.) in diameter from the yellow pre-felt. I placed the petals on the green pre-felt background to form a daisy shape, allowing about ten petals per daisy, and added a yellow circle in the centre of each flower to cover the points where the petals met.

I covered the whole scarf with a piece of net and wetted, soaped and rubbed the scarf until the petals adhered lightly to the green background. Then I removed the net and rolled and finished the scarf in the same way as for the Summer Flowers on page 20.

# summer shimmer

**This beautiful wrap** was made by felting pink fleece to a scarf that I found in a charity shop. Made of pure silk, the scarf was loosely woven with stripes of even more loosely woven fabric every 15cm (6 in.) or so apart. I thought it would be lovely to felt it using the nuno felt technique. This is a one-off wrap – unique and unrepeatable – but if you were to use a silk or viscose wrap in a similar pattern, you would get a similar result.

## Method of felting

First, I placed a towel and bubble wrap on my work surface. with the charity shop scarf on top. Then I laid out pale pink wool fleece on top of the wrap, with all the fibres going in one direction. To create a slightly more interesting effect on the back, I cut lengths of a coordinating cotton and viscose slub knitting yarn about 7.5cm (3 in.) long and placed them randomly on top of the pink fleece, in a strip about 20cm (8 in.) wide and 20cm (8 in.) from the end of the wrap. I added a wisp of pink fleece over the centre of each piece of yarn to 'harness' the piece of yarn to the wrap during the felting process.

Once I was happy with the layout, I placed a net over the whole wrap and wetted, soaped and rubbed the piece until the wool fibres held lightly together. I removed the net, added a second layer of bubble wrap on top and rolled both layers around a swimming noodle. I tied the wrap firmly and rolled it 100 times from each end until the fibres had migrated through the silk fabric and were visible poking through on the other side of the silk. To felt the fibres, I folded the wrap into a parcel and dropped it lightly onto the work surface until it had shrunk to the required size. Finally, I rinsed the wrap in cold water and dried it flat.

# seashore

I've been lucky enough to live near the sea for most of my life and I have

spent many, many hours there, walking the dog, playing with the children –

just watching the sea. I love the way no two beaches are the same.

They all have their own character – and whether it's rocky, sandy – pebbly,

each one is guaranteed to fascinate and inspire me. I probably get more

of my ideas from the sea and the coastline than from anywhere else. All the

projects in this chapter have been inspired by simple things that you can

find on every beach – pebbles, seaweed, shells. These five scarves are all

medium-weight scarves in soft, natural colours.

# white pebbles

**Inspired by** the creamy white pebbles to be found on many beaches, this scarf is made from nuno felt, with the wool felted onto white silk georgette. I took the colours and texture from the pebbles and added a chunky white woollen yarn to form a spiral pattern that occurs so often in nature. If you try to felt this scarf before the fibres have penetrated the silk sufficiently, the wool fibres will just form a layer of felt above the silk, so do check before you begin felting. If the yarn moves around when you push it with your fingertips, it has not adhered sufficiently and needs to be rubbed a little more. This project also introduces the technique of making (intentional!) holes in a piece of nuno felt.

degree of difficulty
✿ ✿ ✿

tools and materials

towel

1 length of bubble wrap, 35 x 204cm (14 x 80 in.)

28 x 198cm (11 x 78 in.) white silk georgette or chiffon

fabric scissors

75g (3 oz) white merino wool tops

small amounts of merino wool tops in several soft colours – light pink, grey, buttermilk and sage

net, 35 x 204cm (14 x 80 in.)

plastic bottle with holes in lid

olive oil soap

small plastic bag

3m (3 yd) 100 per cent wool white slub yarn

sheet of thin plastic, 35 x 204cm (14 x 80 in.)

cane blind

swimming 'noodle' or similar and ties

finished size
20 x 150cm (8 x 59 in.)

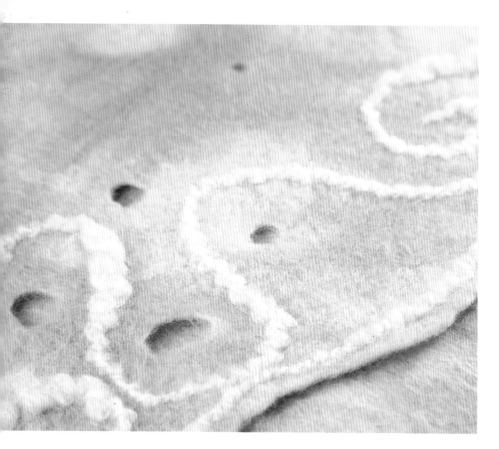

# to make the white pebbles scarf

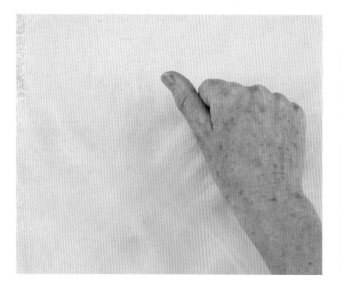

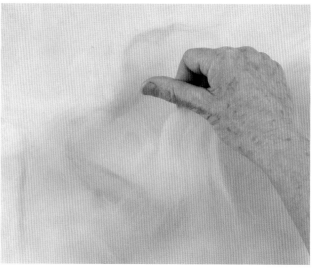

**1** Place the bubble wrap on the towel, with the silk georgette on top. (The silk needs to be about 30 per cent bigger than you want the finished scarf to be, to allow for shrinkage.) Cut a wavy edge along both short ends of the silk. Lay down a fine layer of white merino fibres at random angles, slightly overlapping the edges of the silk.

**2** Lay down a second fine layer of fibres in the same way as the first layer.

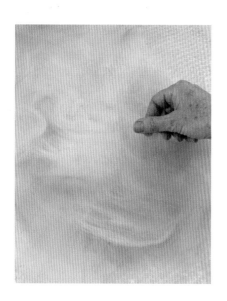

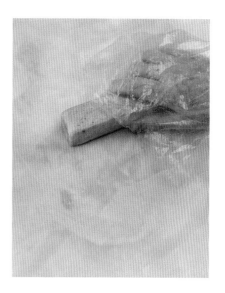

**3** Add the coloured fibres to this layer by placing and mixing them as desired.

**4** Cover the fibres with the net. Starting in the centre and working outwards, gently sprinkle the fibres all over with water. Flatten the surface gently with your hands to help the water soak into the wool fibres.

**5** Gently soap the entire surface, taking care not to dislodge the wool fibres under the net.

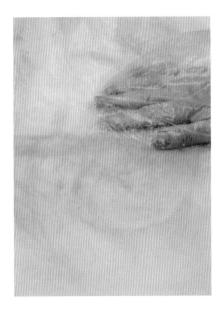

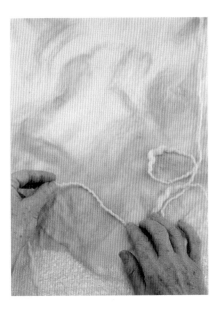

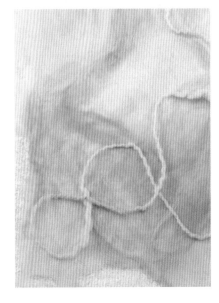

**6** With your hand inside a plastic bag, gently rub the surface in a circular motion until the fibres hold together enough to form a pre-felt (see page 30).

**7** Lift the net and lay on the wool yarn to form a coiling pattern along the length of the scarf and at both ends.

**8** Lightly 'veil' the yarn with tiny wisps of white merino at regular points. This will help the yarn to adhere more firmly to the merino fibres during the felting process.

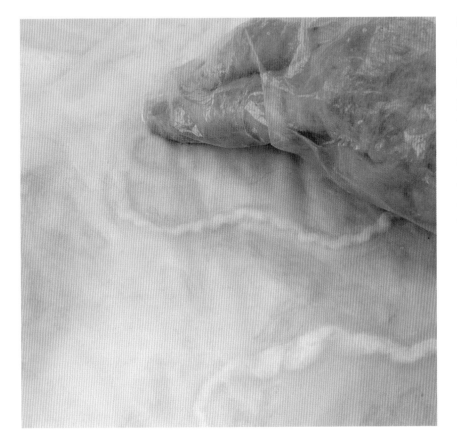

**9** Cover the scarf with net again, then sprinkle water and apply soap along the yarn. Using your fingertips, rub the soap in gently but firmly along the yarn design until it has adhered firmly to the fleece. It is very important to make sure that this has happened before you move onto the next stage, so keep checking by lifting the net and testing with your fingertip. If the yarn moves around freely when you nudge it, you need rub it a little more.

▷

**10** When you are happy that the wool design is firmly in position, place a sheet of thin plastic over the entire scarf and smooth it down so that it clings to the fibres. Lift all three layers – bubble wrap, scarf and plastic – and place them on a cane blind. Roll up around a swimming noodle and tie firmly. Roll 100 times, unroll, straighten, roll up from the other end and roll another 100 times. Repeat until you have rolled the scarf 400 times in total.

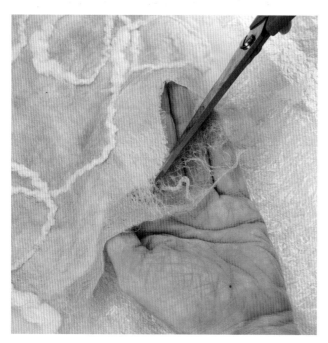

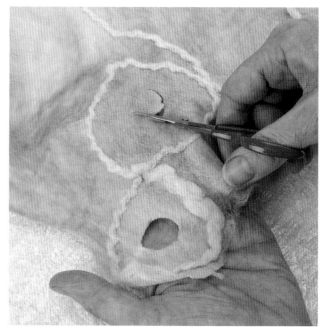

**11** Unroll and look at the silk georgette side of the scarf. If the fibres have worked through the weave evenly along the whole length of the scarf, and if you can pinch and pull them, you can move on to the next step. If not, roll up the scarf again and repeat step 10 until ready. Trim the wavy edges if necessary.

**12** Cut tiny holes where desired for your design. The holes will get bigger during the shrinking process, so don't make them too big. I made them between 0.75 and 1.25cm (¼ and ½ in.) in diameter.

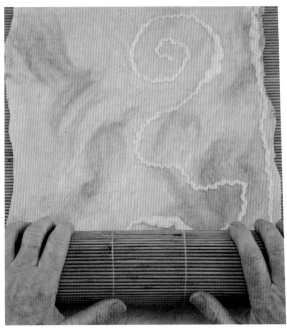

**13** Rub the surface lightly with soap again and sprinkle a little water over it.

**14** Remove the bubble wrap and plastic. Place the scarf on the cane blind, roll it up around the noodle, tie firmly and roll 50 times. Unroll, straighten the scarf, roll it up from the other end, tie and roll a further 50 times

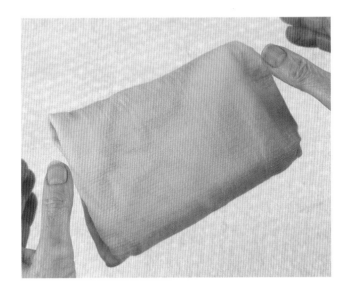

### tip

If you find that the scarf is shrinking very slowly, squeeze out as much water as possible, then place it in a bowl of hot water. Manipulate the scarf gently in the water, then fold it up again quickly and drop it a further 25 times. The heat will speed up the shrinking process; this stage can be repeated until sufficient shrinkage is achieved.

**15** Remove the scarf from the cane blind, fold it into a package with the yarn design on the inside and drop it onto your work surface 25 times. Unwrap the package, straighten the scarf, refold it with yarn still on the inside, and drop it another 25 times. Repeat twice more (several times, if necessary). When the scarf has shrunk enough, rinse it several times in cold water, adding 1 teaspoon of vinegar to the last rinse. Smooth the scarf out, pull it into shape, dry flat and press the back of the scarf with an iron on the wool setting while it is still slightly damp.

# spiral shells

**While on vacation**, I picked up some gorgeous coral-encrusted shells on the beach. The delicate colours and the intricate spiral shape of the shells inspired me to make this pretty scarf.

I chose a soft, natural white background to echo the colour of the sand and a selection of pinks for the shell motifs.

## Method of felting

I began by laying a fine layer of white merino fleece on a piece of silk chiffon measuring roughly 28 x 198cm (11 x 78 in.).

I formed the spirals out of a fingerful of pink fibres from a length of wool tops, a few darker pink fibres and a few lighter fibres. You could make each spiral slightly different by using other combinations of fibres. I twisted the fibres together and wrapped them around one of my fingers to form a spiral, then placed them on top of the fleece.

The scarf was completed in the same way as the White Pebbles scarf on page 44.

# silly seaweed

**Seaweed comes in many shapes and colours –** yellow, green, red, purple. I took the rather unattractively named bladderwrack as my inspiration for this fun scarf and decided to use four different shades of green with an accent of mauve. This project introduces the plastic resist technique of feltmaking, which is used to prevent fleece from felting to itself during rolling when making three-dimensional objects such as bags and hats. Here, it is used to create seaweed 'fronds' that hang free of the main scarf.

degree of difficulty
✿ ✿ ✿

tools and materials

towel

2 sheets of bubble wrap, 30 x 175cm (12 x 68 in.)

1 sheet of bubble wrap, 45cm (18 in.) square

black marker pen

25g (1 oz) of merino wool tops in each of four shades of blue/green

small amount of mauve merino top and tussah silk fibres

net, 30 x 175cm (12 x 68 in.)

plastic bottle with holes in lid

olive oil soap

small plastic bag

templates on pages 126–127

sheets of plastic approximately 30 x 21cm (8 x 12 in.)

swimming 'noodle' or similar and ties

cane blind

finished size

19 x 124cm (7.5 x 49 in.)

# to make the silly seaweed scarf

**1** Lay a sheet of bubble wrap, bubble side down, on the towel. Pull off and lay down a layer of same-colour merino fleece fibres on the bubble wrap, with all the fibres going in the same direction. Cover the bubble wrap, allowing a margin of 2.5 to 5cm (1 to 2 in.) along all sides.

**2** Lay down a second layer of fibres, using several shades of green this time, with each pull of fibres slightly overlapping, but going in random directions.

**3** Place a few tussah silk fibres randomly on top for extra detail and to add a sheen to the surface. You now need to prepare and decorate a second piece in the same colours, approximately 40cm (16 in.) square, out of which you will cut the 'strands' that will be attached to the main scarf.

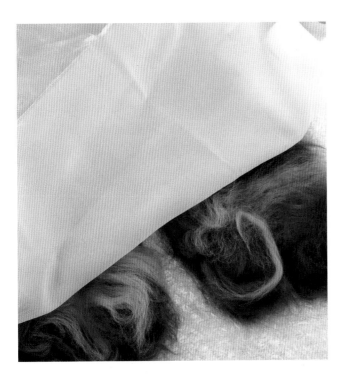

**4** Place a piece of net over both pieces of work.

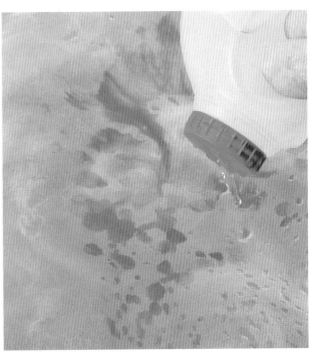

**5** Starting in the centre and working outwards, sprinkle the fibres all over with water. Flatten the surface gently with your hands to help the water soak into the wool fibres.

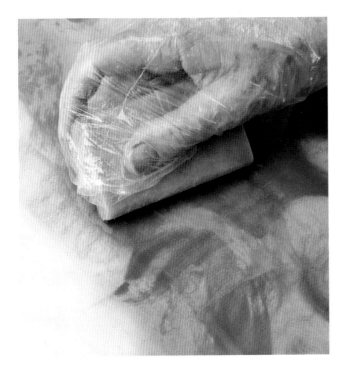

**6** Apply olive oil soap over the net.

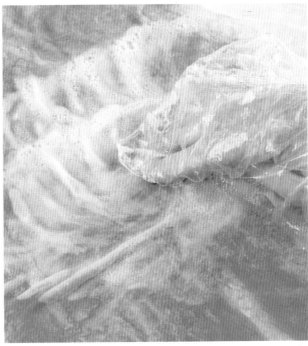

**7** With your hand in a plastic bag, gently rub both pieces until the fibres hold together and have pre-felted.

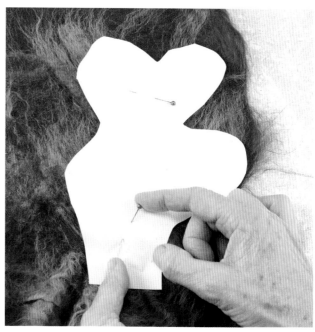

**8** Blot the smaller piece of pre-felt with a towel to remove the excess water.

**9** Copy the templates of the strands and pin them to the smaller piece of pre-felt.

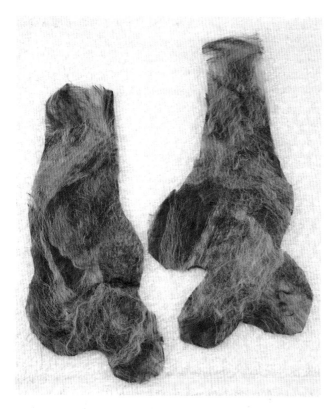

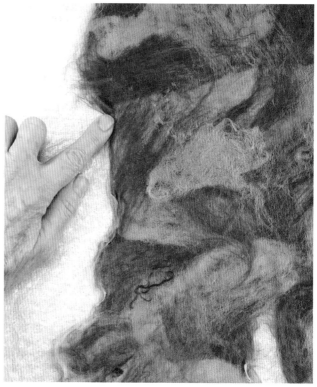

**10** Cut out as many seaweed strands as you wish to add to your scarf.

**11** Tidy up the edges of the scarf by pushing back any stray fibres with your fingertips

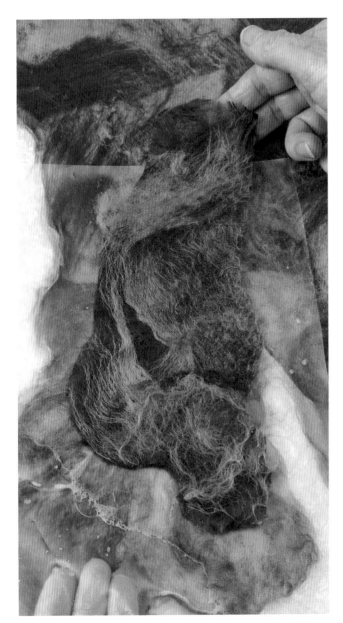

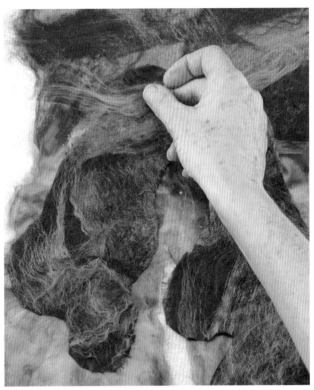

**13** Add a little more fleece above the top 2.5cm (1 in.) of the strands to anchor them securely when felting.

**12** Position the strands towards the end of the scarf. Place a sheet of plastic (I use plastic stationery folders with the edges cut off) underneath each strand, leaving the top 2.5cm (1 in.) of each strand clear of the plastic.

**14** Place the net over the top 2.5cm (1 in.) of the strands and then wet, apply soap and rub gently with your fingertips.

▷

**15** Remove the net and lay the second sheet of bubble wrap over the entire scarf. Roll up both layers around a swimming noodle, tie firmly and roll 100 times.

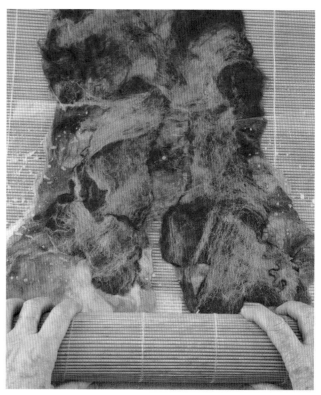

**16** Unroll the scarf, remove the top layer of bubble wrap and reshape the scarf. Re-apply the bubble wrap, roll the scarf up again from the other end and roll 100 times.

**17** Unroll the scarf, remove it from the bubble wrap, and place it on a cane blind. Roll the blind up around a swimming noodle, tie it up and roll 50 times. Unroll, straighten the scarf, roll it up from the other end and roll it another 50 times. Rolling the scarf directly in the cane blind hardens the felt.

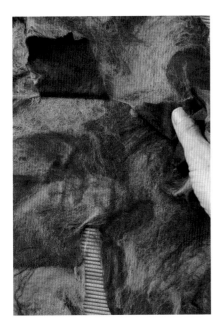

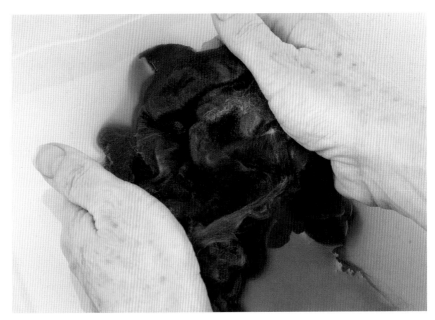

**18** Remove the sheets of plastic from beneath the seaweed strands.

**19** Place the scarf in a bowl of hot water and very gently squeeze and rub it with your fingertips to shrink the fibres together.

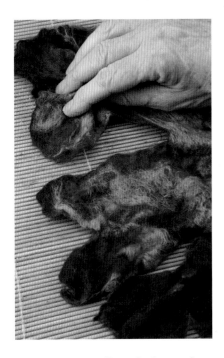

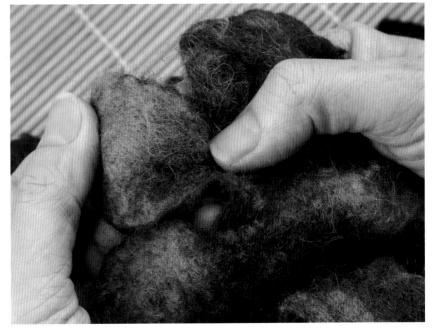

**20** To shrink the fibres further and to shape the scarf, rub the scarf gently against the cane mat, working from one end to the other.

**21** Work at the sides and the seaweed-strand ends of the scarf by squeezing and rubbing them with your fingers to form a wavy edge and a bumpy, seaweed-like surface. Rinse the scarf several times in cold water, adding a few drops of vinegar to the final rinse. Gently squeeze out as much water as possible, reshape the edges and bumps as necessary and dry the scarf flat.

# pebble stripes

**A warm**, **cosy**, **unisex scarf**, this project is easy to make and wear. It was inspired by delicately coloured pebbles whose tones complement each other perfectly: see how the soft shades of grey, beige, sage green, buttermilk and cream occur naturally in the stones.

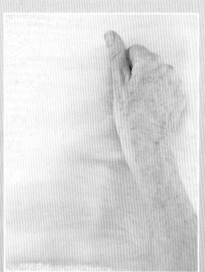

**1** First lay down a layer of cream-coloured fibres horizontally over an area of 24 x 190cm (9.5 x 76 in.).

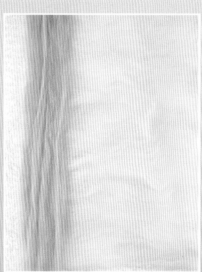

**2** Break off a 190cm (76 in.) length from each of the colours, split each one into four, then place each long strand of fibres on top of the cream fibres.

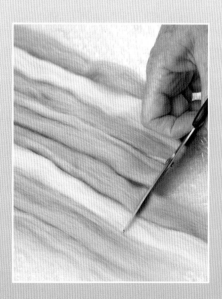

**3** Trim the ends of the fibres, then wet, soap, roll and complete the scarf in the usual way.

# black pebbles

**My favourite beach** is at Crow Point in North Devon – a
wonderful place for beachcombing and a great place to find
driftwood and pebbles of every shape, size and colour. This is where
I found some little smooth black pebbles with thin lines that looked
as if they had been drawn with a fine white pen. I'd never seen such
beautiful pebbles anywhere else and thought the design would
make a simple but very sophisticated scarf.

## Method of felting

I made this scarf by laying out two
even layers of black merino fleece.
On top of this I added several lengths
of a thin, very pale grey knitting yarn
diagonally across the scarf, with
some of the pieces crossing. The
scarf was then wetted, soaped,
rubbed, rolled and completed in
the usual way.

# autumn shades

In autumn, the colours on the trees turn to deep browns, russets and greens and, as the days shorten and the air becomes cooler, the yellows, reds and oranges of fruits and berries appear. Take time to have a close look at autumn leaves. Compare the many beautiful shapes, textures and colours; pick them up and trace around them to make templates and use them in your work. Sometimes the simplest shapes can be the most effective. The scarves in this section are made in rich, warm colours to brighten up even the dullest day and to keep out the chill of those cold, damp mornings.

# sycamore

**This lovely, light scarf** is made from Shetland wool, which is coarser and has a duller finish than merino. Some of the leaves are applied pre-felts and some are machine appliquéd to the finished scarf. I used dupion silk for the appliquéd leaves, as the shine of the fabric contrasts with and complements the soft wool background of the scarf. Make them as rich and as vibrant as possible for a really dramatic effect. The recycled sari silk used for decoration is perfect for incorporating into felt and is available in several different colourways and provides accents of colour and texture.

degree of difficulty

✿ ✿

tools and materials

towel

2 sheets of bubble wrap, 45 x 190cm (18 x 74 in.)

100g (4 oz) natural Shetland wool tops

net, 45 x 190cm (18 x 74 in.)

plastic bottle with holes in lid

olive oil soap

small plastic bag

scraps of merino wool tops and tussah silk in autumn colours

templates on page 125

fabric scissors

3.5 m (3–4 yds) of recycled sari silk

swimming 'noodle' or similar and ties

small piece of silk dupion

small piece of fusible webbing

finished size

26 x 150cm (10 x 58 in.)

# to make the sycamore scarf

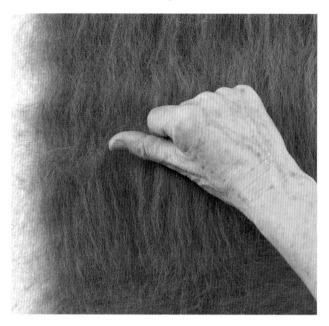

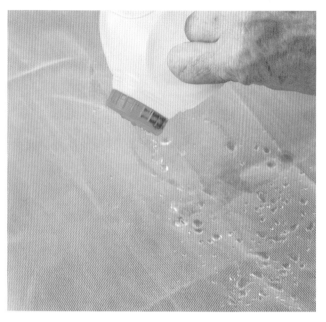

**1** Lay a towel on your work surface, with a piece of bubble wrap on top, bubble side down. Pull out and lay down an even layer of natural Shetland wool fibres in the centre of the bubble wrap, covering an area 35 x 190cm (13.5 x 74 in.), with all the fibres lying horizontally. Lay out a second layer with the fibres at right angles to the first.

**2** Cover the fibres with the net. Starting in the centre and working outwards, sprinkle the fibres all over with water. Flatten the surface gently with your hands to help the water soak into the wool fibres.

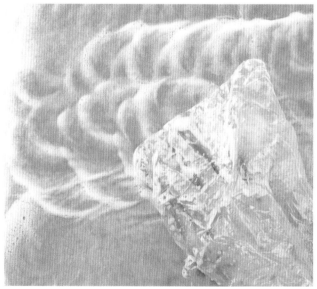

**3** Apply soap evenly over the entire scarf, working your way from one end to the other.

**4** With your hand in a plastic bag, gently rub the fibres in a circular motion, working your way from one end of the scarf to the other, until the fibres hold together to form a pre-felt (see page 30).

**5** Make three or four small pre-felts 13–15cm (5–6 in.) square from merino wool tops in contrasting colours. I made four pre–felts – one in gold, one in burgundy and rich reds, one in browns and greens, and one in mixed browns.

**6** Cut out the templates and pin them to the pre-felts. Cut out a selection of leaves in varying colours.

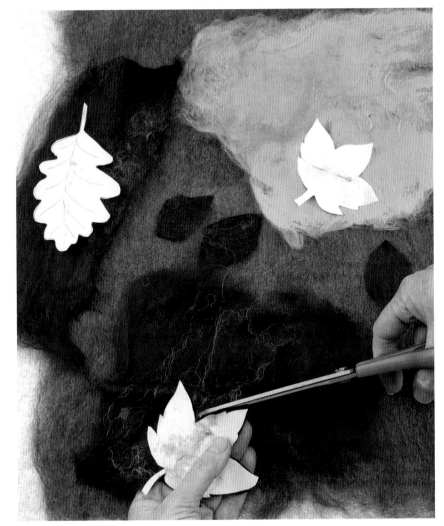

tip
Templates can be cut from dry or from damp pre-felts.

**7** Take a couple of lengths of spun recycled sari silk and lay them along the length of the pre-felted scarf. Place the cut-out leaves in position. Lay several leaves, just touching each other, along the short ends of the scarf.

**8** When you are happy with the design, put the net over the scarf, sprinkle on some water and gently apply soap to the leaves and along the entire length of the yarn.

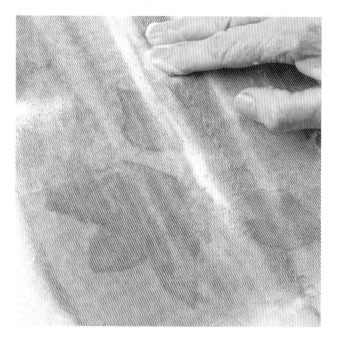

**9** Very gently rub the leaves and the area just around them and all along the yarn, with your fingertips. This will help the leaves and the yarn adhere to the scarf fibres before felting. Peel back the net and check that all the leaves are holding in place and that the yarn is lightly holding to the fibres. This is very important: if they are not holding, they may move around during the rolling process. When all the leaves and the yarn are holding fast, tidy the edges by pushing any stray fibres back with your fingertips. Place another sheet of bubble wrap over the scarf, roll it up firmly around a swimming noodle, tie and roll it backwards and forwards 50 times. Unroll, pull the scarf to shape, roll it up again from the other end and roll another 50 times. Repeat this twice more. By checking every 50 rolls, you have more control over what is happening during the felting process.

**10** After you have rolled 200 times in total, cut around the leaf shapes at each end of the scarf to give a shaped edge, then roll the scarf up and roll it again. When you have rolled another 200 times, your scarf may be ready. If it is not, roll it up again and repeat the rolling step. Rinse the scarf in warm water, gently manipulating it to felt the fibres a little more. Rinse the scarf several times in cold water, adding a few drops of vinegar to the last rinse. Pull the scarf into shape and dry flat. Iron on the back while still damp, with the iron on the wool setting, if required.

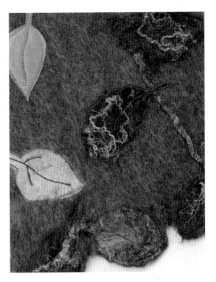

**11** While the scarf is drying, prepare the leaves for machine appliqué. Following the manufacturer's instructions, apply fusible webbing to the back of the dupion silk, then cut out the required number of leaves.

**12** Peel off the backing from the fusible webbing, then position the leaves on the scarf where required. Carefully iron the leaves in place, using an iron on the wool setting.

**13** Machine stitch around the leaf shapes to appliqué them to the scarf. Stitch around all the other leaves to give them more definition.

# falling leaves

**This scarf is a fun accessory**, guaranteed to add a splash of colour to any outfit. Made using very thick knitting yarn that comes in a fabulous range of colours, it reminds me of leaves as they fall from the trees. I make this scarf in all sorts of colours: here I've used a tiger-stripe combination (see opposite) and mix of coral and sea plant colours (page 77), as well as the pinks and purples in the scarf below.

degree of difficulty

tools and materials

towel

2 sheets of bubble wrap, 30 x 132cm (12 x 52 in.)

30g (1½ oz) purple merino wool tops

100g (4 oz) hank of chunky slub wool yarn in autumn shades

plastic bottle with holes in lid

olive oil soap

small plastic bag

swimming 'noodle' or similar and ties

cane blind

finished length

120cm (47 in.)

# to make the falling leaves scarf

**1** Lay a piece of bubble wrap, bubble side up, on a towel. Break off a length of fibres the size that you want the scarf to be, plus about 30 per cent to allow for shrinkage. (I used a length 170cm/67 in. long.) Split the length evenly into three strands. (You will only use two of these strands.)

**2** Cut the hank of wool yarn into 35–40 pieces 18–20cm (7–8 in.) long.

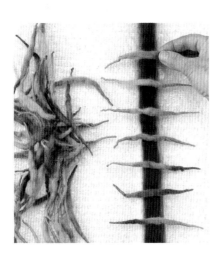

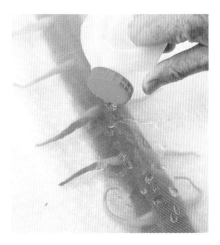

**3** Lay one strand of merino wool fibre down the centre of the bubble wrap, opening the fibres up so that it forms a strip about 2cm (¾ in.) wide. Lay the short lengths of yarn evenly across the strip at 5cm (2-in.) intervals.

**4** Place the second long strand of fibres that you made in Step 1 directly on top of the first, sandwiching the shorter yarn lengths in between.

**5** Lay a piece of net over the entire scarf, sprinkle with cold water and flatten with your hands to help the water soak into the wool fibres.

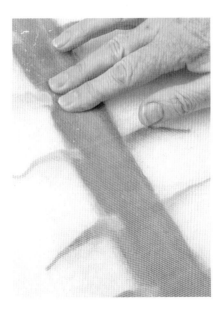

**6** Gently rub the long strand of fibres with soap.

**7** Using your fingertips, rub along the length of the strand, paying particular attention to places where the yarn crosses the strand. Do not start rolling until all these areas hold firm.

**8** Lift the net occasionally to check that the fibres are not sticking to the net. If the fibres on the long strand have spread, push them back into position.

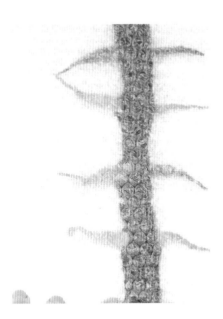

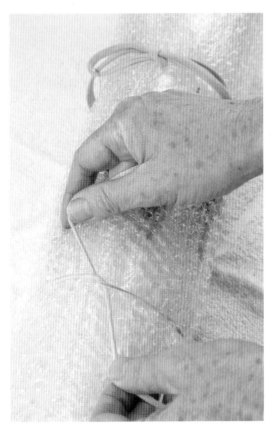

**10** Roll up the scarf around a swimming noodle, tie firmly and roll 100 times. Unroll, stretch out the scarf (again making sure that the short strands of yarn are not touching), roll up from the other end, tie and roll another 100 times. Repeat this step until the long central strand of wool fibres is completely felted.

**9** Place another piece of bubble wrap, smooth side up, on top of the scarf, making sure that none of the short strands of yarn are touching each other or they will felt together.

**11** Remove the scarf from the bubble wrap, place it on a cane blind and gently rub the whole scarf against the panels of the blind, thus working the fibres together a little more.

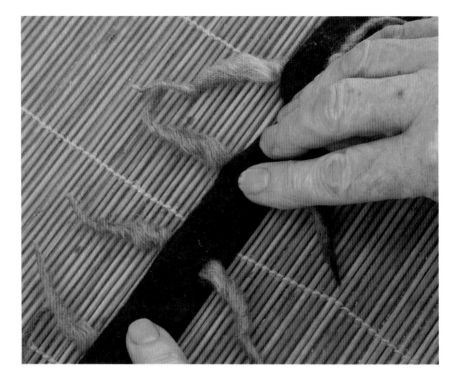

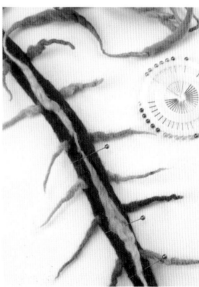

**12** Gently roll the scarf between your hands to encourage the fibres to felt more, making sure that the short strands of yarn do not touch each other and felt together.

**13** Place the scarf in a bowl of hot water and gently rub the long strand of fibres so that it shrinks a little more. Rinse several times in cold water, adding a few drops of vinegar to the final rinse. Squeeze out as much water as possible, stretch the scarf lengthwise and dry flat.

**14** You may find that despite all your efforts some of the short strands of yarn are still a little loose. To rectify this and to add a final touch, when the scarf is dry, place a length of the wool yarn down the centre of the scarf, pin it in place and machine stitch over it using a zigzag stitch.

## variation

You could create several of these simple-to-make little scarves in different colours to jazz up your wardrobe. This version reflects the colour of the ocean and the delicate shades of the corals and plants found beneath the sea. Wear it during the cold, wet winter months to remind you that summer is not far away!

# moorland

**The natural curls** of the Wensleydale sheep give this gorgeous warm scarf loads of interest and texture and add a tactile quality. The deep, rich colours can be found in the flowering heather on moor and heathland and in the bracken and gorse as they turn to a deeper brown as autumn progresses. If you look carefully at the leaves you will see a range of shades of brown, purple, and reds that you would not necessarily think of putting together, but which complement each other perfectly.

## Method of felting

I began by laying out two layers of burgundy fibres, with a strip of purple fibres about 2cm (¾ in.) wide along the edges and the ends of the top layer. After teasing the Wensleydale curls apart, I placed them on the scarf so that about 12cm (4½ in.) of the scarf was covered at each short end, carefully separating the curls to form a fringe.

Then I placed a net over the scarf, and wetted, soaped, and gently rubbed the scarf all over, paying particular attention to the areas where the Wensleydale fibres cover the scarf. It's important not to start rolling until these fibres have adhered to the fibres beneath. This may take a little time, as the Wensleydale fibres are quite shiny and slippery. When the Wensleydale fringe fibres had adhered firmly to the merino fibres, I rolled and completed the scarf in the same way as the Summer Flowers scarf on page 20.

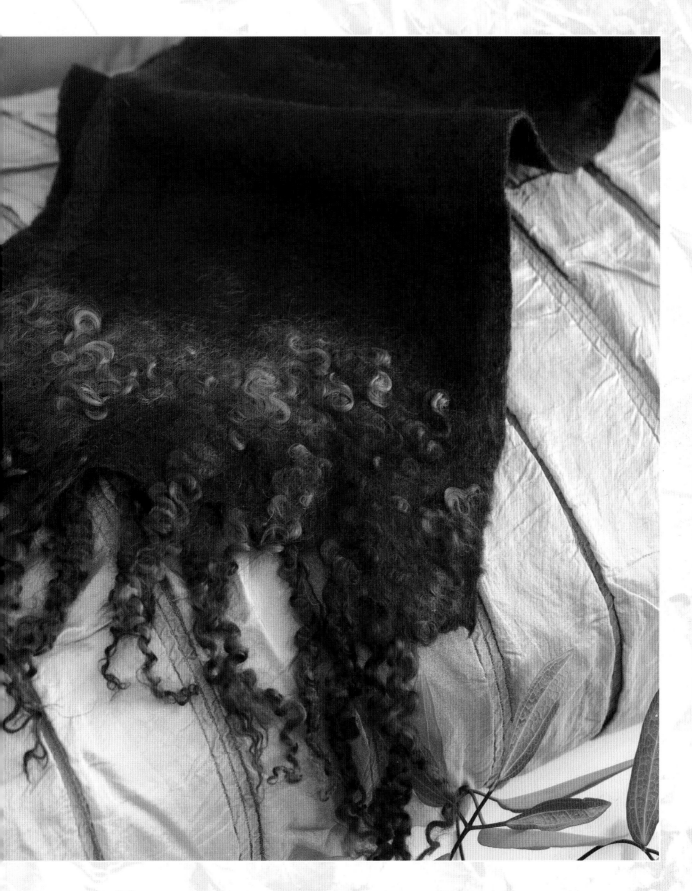

# raindrops

**This is a soft**, **cosy scarf** with silk 'raindrops' to lighten the autumn colours. The scarf is made in exactly the same way as the Summer Flowers scarf on page 20, but instead of the white silk flowers I cut raindrop motifs from an old patterned viscose scarf that I found in a charity shop. The lovely mix of coloured fleece and white silk was purchased already carded.

## Method of felting

To create this scarf, I made a raindrop template and cut out several raindrops from a viscose scarf. I placed five or six of these motifs evenly at each end of the scarf, then wet, soaped, and completed the scarf using the same method as the Summer Flowers scarf on page 20.

# cobweb

**Autumn is the time for vibrant colours** and cold, frosty mornings, with intricately spun, dewy cobwebs adorning the plants and hedgerows. This delicate scarf combines the feel of cobwebs with the colours of the turning leaves.

## Method of felting

I began by placing two wavy lines of thick knitting yarn along the length of the bubble wrap. On top, I added as fine a layer as possible of marine blue fibres, with a very fine layer of burgundy fibres on top of that, at right angles to the blue layer. Then I placed lengths of knitting yarn on top of the wool fibres to echo the design on the underside of the wrap.

To felt the fibres, I placed a net over them, then wetted, soaped, and rubbed gently until the fibres held together and the knitting yarn adhered lightly to the merino fibres. I rolled the scarf first in bubble wrap and then in a cane blind until all the fibres had felted firmly together. To complete the scarf, I pulled it back into shape lengthwise, rinsed it and dried it flat.

# woodlands

Stroll through any woodland at any time of year and you'll find inspiration.

In winter, without the foliage, it's easier to focus on the colours and textures

of the trees themselves. In spring, there are the fresh greens of the new

leaves and often a carpet of wild flowers on the ground. In summer, the

greens soften and the wild flowers present a different colourway; and in fall

we're treated to a whole new palette of colours – yellows, browns, rust,

burgundy and red. The scarves and wraps in this chapter reflect that variety:

scarves in fresh, natural colours; lightweight scarves in fresh spring greens;

and warmer ones in richer colours for later in the year.

# mossy green

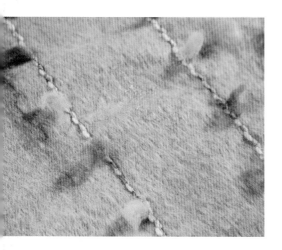

**This scarf brings to mind** the fresh green of the soft moss that carpets and cushions the ground and grows up the walls and trees in the woods. It is a very lightweight cobweb scarf, with a touch of texture added by stitching on rows of fancy knitting yarn after the felting is finished.

## degree of difficulty
✿ ✿

### tools and materials

towel

cane blind

bubble wrap, 40 x 165cm (15 x 65 in.)

50g (2 oz) fresh green merino wool tops

scraps of green silk tussah

net, 40 x 165cm (15 x 65 in.)

plastic bottle with holes in lid

olive oil soap

small plastic bag

sheet of very thin plastic, at least 165cm (65 in.) long

swimming 'noodle' or similar and ties

### finished size

20 x 122cm (8 x 48 in.)

## to make the mossy green scarf

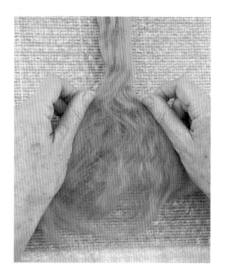

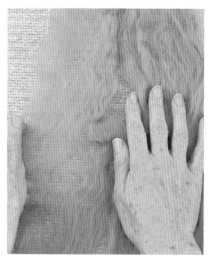

**1** Lay a cane blind on the towel with a sheet of bubble wrap on top, bubble side down. Break off green merino wool fibres the length of the finished scarf plus about 30 per cent extra to allow for shrinkage. (I used a length about 160cm/62 in. long.) Place the wool on the bubble wrap and spread out the fibres.

**2** Starting at one end and working downwards, spread the fibres out as finely and as evenly as possible trying not to leave any gaps.

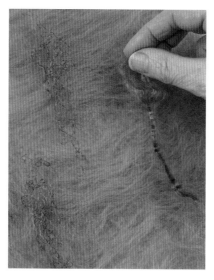

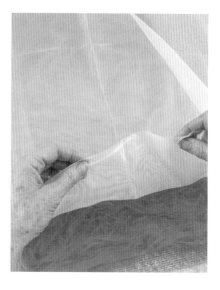

**3** Pull off several lengths of merino tops the width of the fibres laid down in step 2. Spread them horizontally across the first layer of fibres. This layer can be even finer than the first.

**4** Place some wisps of tussah silk randomly on the wool fibres.

**5** Cover the fibres with net, taking care not to dislodge the fibres.

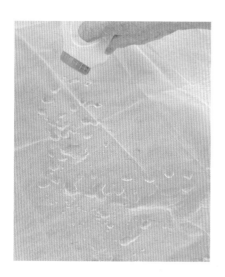

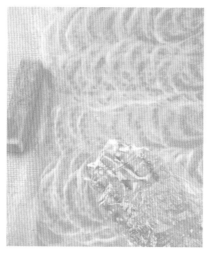

**6** Starting in the centre and working outwards, sprinkle the fibres all over with water. Flatten the surface gently with your hands to help the water soak into the wool fibres. Spread olive oil soap over the net.

**7** With your hand inside a plastic bag, rub the surface all over. Do not let the fibres work their way through the net, because it will be very difficult to remove them from the net without damage. Remove the net, tidy the edges of the scarf and place a sheet of plastic over the entire scarf.

**8** Place a swimming noodle on top of the fibres, then roll all the layers up tightly together.

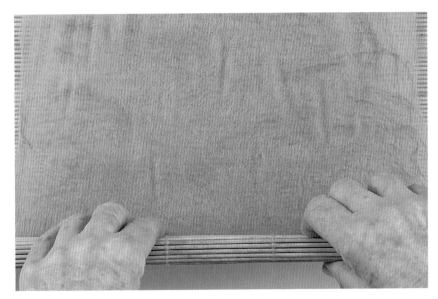

**9** Tie up firmly and roll 100 times. Unroll, carefully straighten the scarf and repeat, this time rolling from the other end. Repeat until the scarf has been rolled 400 times in total. Remove the scarf from the bubble wrap and plastic and place it directly on the cane blind. Roll it up, tie, roll 50 times, unroll, pull it into shape, roll it up from the other end and roll 50 times. Repeat so that the scarf has been rolled a total of 200 times in the cane blind.

**10** Roll one end of the scarf in one end of the blind and the other end into the opposite end of the blind. Holding both rolled-up ends firmly, pull evenly to stretch the scarf. (If your scarf is very long, get someone to help you.) Wet and soap the scarf again and continue to roll it until the fibres hold together very firmly. Rinse the scarf several times in cold water, adding a few drops of vinegar to the final rinse, stretch and dry flat.

**11** When the scarf is dry, decorate it by pinning three lengths of fancy knitting yarn along the length, then stitch over the yarn, using a zigzag stitch on the sewing machine.

# forest green

This is a double-sided scarf in glorious green. It was inspired by the colour of some dyed Wensleydale curls that I came across, which reminded me of the greens found in woodlands. Sometimes, just looking at fibres and colours is enough to inspire a project. The materials for this scarf were gathered in just this way. I used merino fleece in a deep green to match the Wensleydale curls and added a touch of green tussah silk for extra sparkle and surface interest.

degree of difficulty
✿

tools and materials

towel

2 sheets of bubble wrap, 45 x 188cm (18 x 74 in.)

100g (4 oz) deep green merino wool tops

dyed tussah silk fibres

25g (1 oz) dyed Wensleydale curls

net, 45 x 188cm (18 x 74 in.)

plastic bottle with holes in lid

olive oil soap

small plastic bag

swimming 'noodle' or similar and ties

finished size

28 x 130cm (11 x 51 in.)

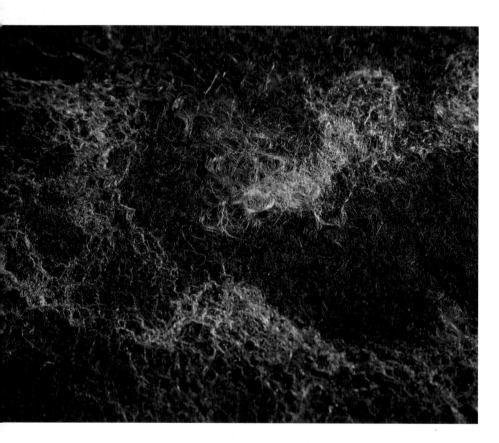

# to make the forest green scarf

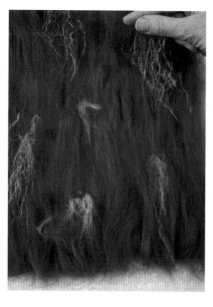

**1** Lay a towel on your work surface, with bubble wrap on top, bubble side down. Lay down two layers of wool fibres at right angles to each other.

**2** Pull off wisps of silk fibres and lay them down on the scarf, positioning them randomly.

**3** Place Wensleydale curls at regular intervals along both short ends of the scarf, spacing them about 6cm (2½ in.) apart to form a fringe.

**4** In order to decorate the other side of the scarf and make it double-sided, you need to turn the work over. To do this, place the second piece of bubble wrap on the scarf, smooth side down.

**5** Smooth your hands along the scarf to compress the fibres a little and to keep everything in place. Take hold of one side and flip the scarf over. Remove the top layer of bubble wrap and repeat steps 2 and 3.

**6** Along the short ends, place Wensleydale curls in the spaces left between the curls on the first side, to form an even fringe.

**7** Cover the fibres with the net, making sure that the fringe pieces do not touch each other. Starting in the centre and working outwards, sprinkle the fibres with cold water. Flatten the surface with your hands to help the water soak into the fibres.

**8** Gently apply soap to the entire scarf.

**9** With your hand inside a plastic bag, gently rub the whole scarf. Take particular care to rub the edges so that the merino and Wensleydale fibres hold together. Do not rub the fringes themselves too much, as you want them to remain soft and curly.

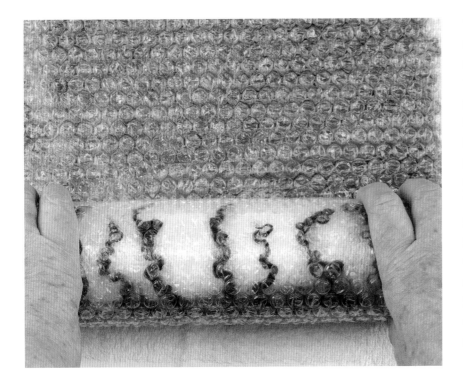

**10** Place the second piece of bubble wrap over the scarf, roll it up around a swimming noodle, tie firmly and roll 100 times. Unroll, reshape the scarf and check that the strands of the fringes aren't touching each other. Roll up again from the other end and roll another 100 times. Repeat until you have rolled 600 times in total. The fibres should now be holding together firmly. If they are not, repeat the rolling stage. Remove the scarf from the bubble wrap and pull it into shape. Rinse the scarf several times in cold water, adding a few drops of vinegar to the last rinse. Dry flat and iron on the back with a medium iron.

# beech tree nuno

**The idea for this design** came from my observations of a beech leaf – a simple shape, yet very effective. This is a nuno felt scarf, in which a very fine layer of wool fibres is felted onto a backing of silk chiffon to produce a lightweight but strong fabric.

## Method of felting

I began by placing a very fine layer of wool and silk fibres on a piece of white silk chiffon cut to size. Then I made a pre-felt (see page 30) about 25cm (10 in.) square, using greens with a little pink, gold and blue for interest. I cut out 15–20 leaves from the pre-felt, using the beech leaf template on page 124, and laid them on the scarf where required. At each short end of the scarf, I added a row of leaves just touching each other. In the spaces left, I included little scraps of thread, silk and yarn for decoration. Once the design had been laid out, I covered it with polyester voile and wetted, soaped and rubbed it until the fibres were firm and beginning to migrate through to the other side of the chiffon. The scarf was completed in the usual way.

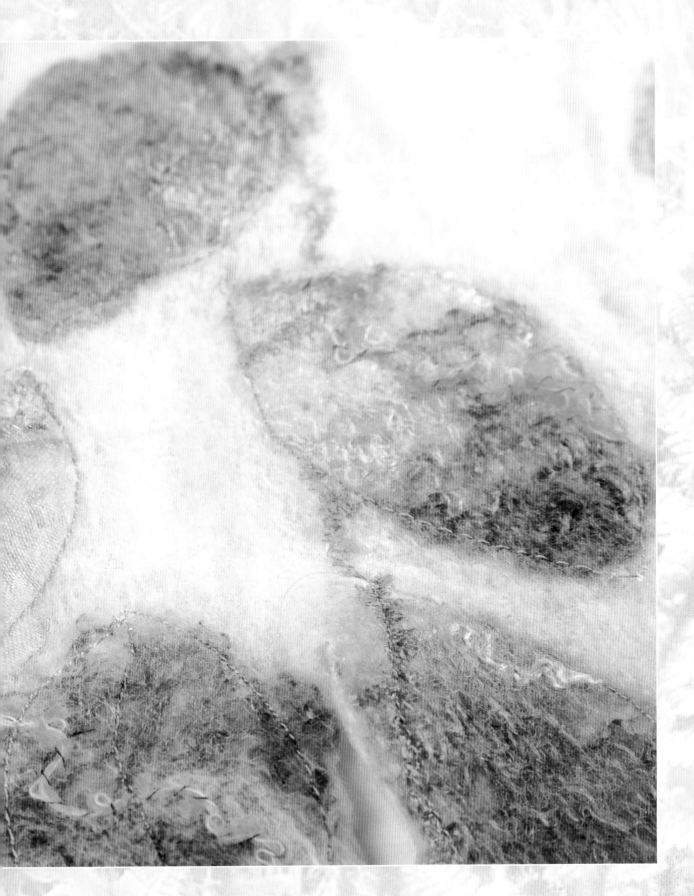

# treebark

**Made from wool** from the Black Welsh sheep carded with silk, this scarf is very light. A contrast to the fresh greens of the woodlands, it reminds me of the texture and colour of bark. The decoration was provided by a fancy knitting yarn that I've had for years, which is ideal for bringing a touch of colour and texture to a woodland or moorland scene. The scarf is very simple to make, but very effective.

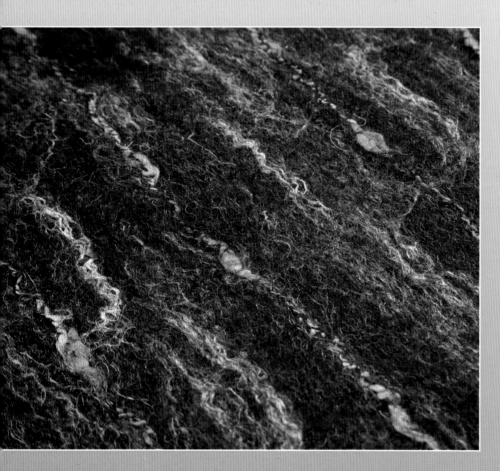

### Method of felting

First, I marked out the size of the scarf on a piece of bubble wrap, adding 25–30 per cent extra to allow for shrinkage. Then I cut a few lengths of fancy yarn and arranged them in coil patterns on the bubble wrap. Two layers of fibres were placed on top of the yarn designs at right angles to each other, then three or four lengths of yarn were added along the length of the top layer of fibres, spacing them evenly. The scarf was then covered with net and wetted, soaped and completed in the same way as the Sycamore scarf on page 66.

# woodland wrap

**This pretty wrap is** made from Blue-faced Leicester wool and the colours remind me of the sunlight as it filters through the trees. This wool is very easy to felt and, as the fibres have a natural curl, it produces a very soft and slightly textured felt. I used a fancy knitting yarn and dyed Wensleydale curls to decorate the wrap.

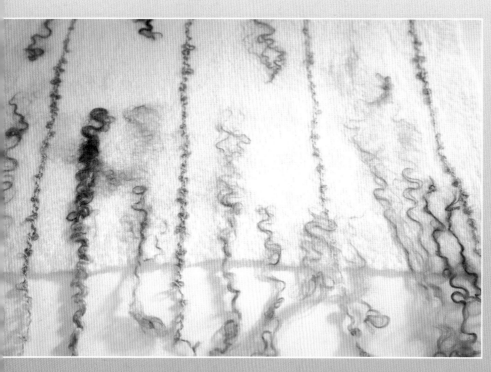

### Method of felting

On bubble wrap I marked out an area roughly 76 x 205cm (30 x 80 in.) and laid down two layers of Blue-faced Leicester wool fibres at right angles to each other. I then placed four lengths of fancy yarn along the length of the scarf, spacing them evenly. For the decorative fringe, I carefully pulled off some Wensleydale curls, teased them apart and placed them over the short ends of the wrap, leaving about 7.5cm (3 in.) between each one. I also positioned a few curls randomly along the wrap.

Finally, I covered the piece with net, wetted, soaped, rubbed and completed the wrap in the same way as the Sycamore scarf on page 66.

# tropical

I think I fell in love with the Caribbean the moment I stepped off the plane

on my first visit. The colours, the climate, the light, the sounds, the

people – and maybe most of all, the everchanging shades of the ocean

and the beautiful clear water full of fish, coral, shells, and plants.

Wool is not normally the first fiber you would think of for the tropics,

but the lightweight scarves and wraps in this section will provide just what

you need on those chillier evenings when the Trade Winds blow. And, as

the colours of the fibers stay so pure throughout the felting process, wool

is perfect for reproducing the vibrant tropical colours and textures.

# ocean wrap

**In the Caribbean**, the colour of the water is a deep marine blue, with flecks of white here and there, where little waves break. I thought it would be great to try to capture this effect in a wrap. I added a sea anemone pin as a finishing touch (see page 106).

This wrap is made not in the usual way, with laid-out wool fibres, but with mohair knitting yarn. You can felt any yarn successfully in this way provided it is made of at least 75 per cent wool fibres. Mohair felts excellently as it is so hairy! I used a 75 per cent mohair, 25 per cent viscose yarn and the viscose gives the white fleck.

## degree of difficulty
❀ ❀

## tools and materials

towel

2 sheets of bubble wrap, 45 x 190cm
  (18 x 75 in.)

black marker pen

4 x 25g (1 oz.) balls of
  mohair/viscose knitting yarn

net curtain fabric, 45 x 190cm
  (18 x 75 in.)

plastic bottle with holes in lid

olive oil soap

small plastic bag

swimming 'noodle' or similar and ties

tiny pearl beads

sewing kit

## finished size

40 x 138cm (16 x 54 in.)

## to make the ocean wrap

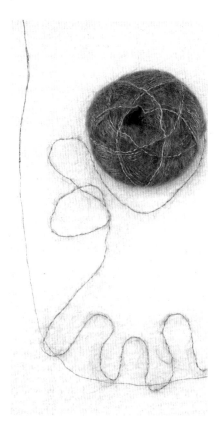

**1** Lay down a sheet of bubble wrap on top of a towel, smooth side up. Using a black marker pen, mark out the shape of the wrap, adding 15–20 per cent extra to allow for shrinkage. (This wrap won't shrink as much as normal felting.) I marked out an area roughly 46 x 156cm (18 x 61 in.). Unwind the yarn and lay it randomly on the marked-out area in such a way that the yarn constantly criss-crosses itself.

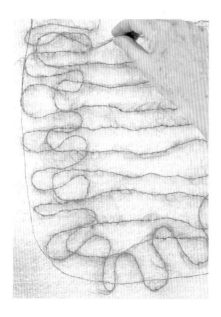

**2** Start at one end, working around the edge of the entire design in a figure-of-eight movement. Fill in the middle, until you have an even layer of fibres crossing over each other.

**3** When you have completed one layer, add another in the same way, making sure that the layers are of as even a thickness as possible.

**4** Continue laying out your yarn until you have a thick and even network of wool over the entire area.

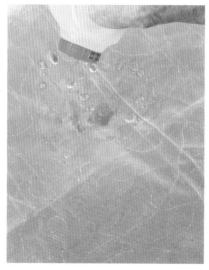

**5** When you are happy with the layout, place a piece of net curtain fabric over the fibres.

**6** Starting at the centre and working outwards, sprinkle the fibres with cold water and gently flatten the surface with your hands so that the fibres absorb the water.

**7** Carefully apply soap over the whole wrap. With your hand in a plastic bag, gently rub over the whole surface in a circular motion for several minutes, paying particular attention to the edge of the wrap.

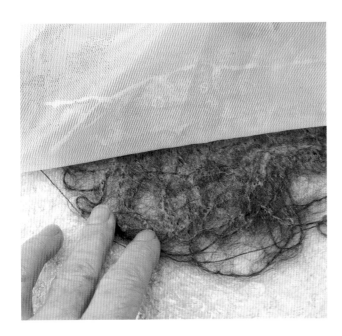

**8** Check under the net at regular intervals while you are rubbing to make sure the edges of the wrap remain nice and tight; if you find that they are spreading, gently push the fibres back with your fingers. It is very important to make sure that all the fibres are holding together well before you begin to roll.

**9** Place another piece of bubble wrap, smooth side down, on top of your design. Roll the layers up firmly around a swimming noodle, tie and roll 50 times. Unwrap, remove the top layer of bubble wrap and reshape the wrap. Replace the bubble wrap and roll the wrap up again, this time from the other end. Roll another 50 times. Repeat this step again. After you have rolled 200 times, the fibres should be sufficiently felted to hold together permanently; but if they are not, repeat the rolling process 50 times each way. Rinse the wrap several times in cold water, adding a few drops of vinegar to the final rinse. Carefully pull the wrap into shape, dry flat and iron the back with the iron set to medium heat.

**10** Decorate the wrap by stitching on tiny pearl beads here and there to give it a little sparkle, like sunlight glinting on the ocean.

# anemone pin

## degree of difficulty
❀

### tools and materials

20g (½ oz) merino wool tops to match mohair yarn in the Ocean Wrap

few scraps of mauve merino tops

bubble wrap

plastic bottle with holes in lid

liquid soap

olive oil soap

brooch clasp or pin

**An anemone pin** adds a finishing touch to the Ocean Wrap. I made this one in the same colours as the wrap, but you could use a variety of colours to create a more vibrant anemone.

## to make the sea anemone pin

**1** Break the merino tops into lengths of about 20cm (8 in.) and split each length into six.

**2** Place the bubble wrap bubble side up, with one of the fibre lengths on top. Sprinkle with water to which you have added a little liquid soap.

**3** Gently roll the fibres into a sausage shape, applying more pressure as the fibres begin to hold together

**4** To add more soap to assist the felting process, rub olive oil soap over the bubble wrap and roll the sausage over the soapy surface.

**5** Roll the sausage in your hands until it is quite firm. Repeat the process with all the lengths of fibres, then rinse and dry.

**6** When they are dry, fold each length in half and stitch them together at the fold to form the anemone.

**7** Finally, stitch a brooch pin to the back. If you wish, stitch a couple of tiny pearl beads to the centre of the pin for a little extra sparkle.

# underwater

**This nuno scarf is gossamer fine**, for those summer evenings when you just need the lightest thing to wrap around your shoulders. With a row of delicate starfish at each end and fish swimming up and down it, it captures the feel of the Caribbean: you can almost feel the warm water lapping at your feet when you hold it!

This scarf is not for the inexperienced or the impatient! As a general rule, the finer the felt, the more difficult it is to make – and this scarf is very, very fine. The best base fabric to use is silk tulle; as it is a natural fibre, the wool fibres will attach themselves to it more successfully and faster than to a manmade fibre. A less expensive option is a soft polyester tulle or net, but you will have to roll the scarf many more times to ensure that the fibres migrate through the fabric. You could also use silk georgette or chiffon, which is cheaper than the silk tulle but will not give such a 'see-through' effect.

degree of difficulty
✿ ✿ ✿

tools and materials

cane blind

towel

bubble wrap, 45 x 188cm (18 x 74 in.)

silk tulle, chiffon or georgette, 38 x 182cm (15 x 72 in.)

50g (2 oz) white merino wool tops

white silk tussah fibres

scraps of pastel merino tops and tussah silk for motifs

fancy pastel yarns and threads for decoration, preferably natural fibres

polyester voile, 45 x 188cm (18 x 74 in.)

water spray

liquid soap

small plastic bag

very thin plastic, 45 x 188cm (18 x 74 in.)

templates on page 125

fabric scissors

swimming 'noodle' or similar and ties

finished size

29 x 150cm (11 x 60 in.)

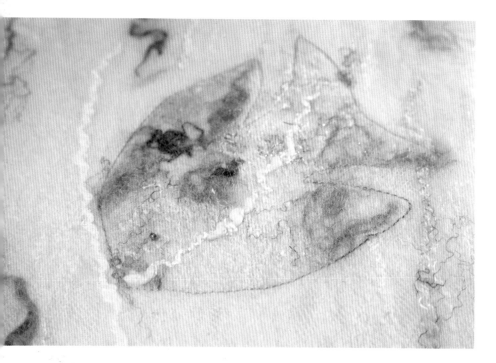

# to make the underwater scarf

**1** Lay a cane blind on the towel with a piece of bubble wrap, bubble side down, on top. Place a piece of very fine soft silk tulle or similar, cut to size, on the bubble wrap. Gently pull off and lay down the finest layer possible of white merino fleece over the whole of the piece of tulle. Make sure you have an even layer along the edges. Pull off wisps of white silk tussah and place them randomly over the white merino.

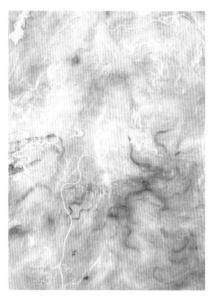

**2** On a separate piece of bubble wrap, prepare two pre-felts (see page 30) about 30cm (12 in.) square in pastel-coloured merino. I used a combination of white and very pale mauves, blues and greens, laid down in two layers and topped with a fine layer of tussah silk in similar colours to the merino fibres beneath.

**3** Drop in a few strands of threads and fancy yarns. Place polyester voile over the fibres. As the layers are so delicate, apply the water using a spray (as opposed to a sprinkler) so as not to disturb the fibres, adding a little liquid soap to the water. When the fibres are wet, apply olive oil soap very gently. With your hand in a plastic bag, rub until the fibres hold together. Blot with a towel to remove some of the moisture.

**4** Cut out templates and pin them to the pre-felts. Using the fabric scissors, cut out 12–15 motifs. If you find that the pre-felts are drying out and are difficult to handle and cut, spray them with a little more water.

**5** Place the motifs where desired on the scarf. In order not to disturb the fine layer of background fibres, gently spray the scarf with water and then position the motifs. If you place motifs along each of the short edges of the scarf, they will form a firm edge when felting.

**6** When you have positioned all the motifs, place a few lengths of fancy yarns on the scarf.

**7** Place a few wisps of tussah silk in the spaces evenly along the length of the scarf.

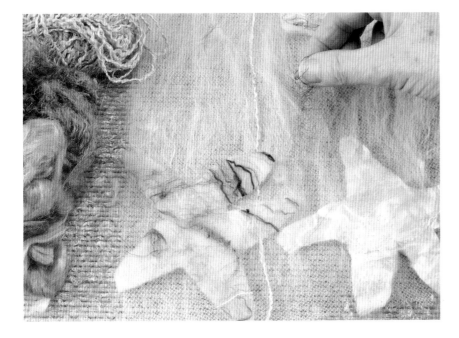

**8** Place a piece of polyester voile over the entire scarf. I use polyester voile in preference to net when making very fine felt, as I find the fibres adhere less than they do to net during the rubbing process

**9** Spray again with water, paying special attention to the areas where there is a motif or a length of yarn.

**10** Very gently apply soap and, with your hand in a plastic bag, rub in a circular motion. Lift the voile regularly to check that the fibres are not sticking to it. Make sure that all the areas of design are holding to the fibres and beginning to migrate through the fabric before you move onto the rolling process.

**11** Remove the voile and place a sheet of thin plastic over the scarf.

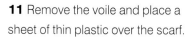

**12** Roll up the scarf, inside the cane blind, bubble wrap and plastic, around a swimming noodle, tie firmly and roll 200 times. Unroll, reshape the scarf, roll it up again from the other end and roll another 200 times. Unroll and check to see if the fibres have migrated through the fabric. If they have not, repeat the rolling process. Do not move on to the next stage until you are sure that the fibres have attached themselves firmly to the fabric over the whole scarf, particularly along the edges.

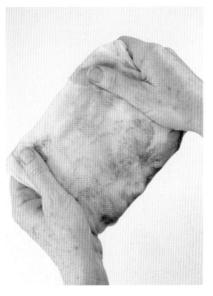

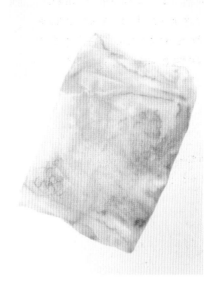

**13** Remove the scarf from the bubble wrap and cane blind. Reshape it and trim any excess fabric from around the end motifs if necessary. Add a little more soap and water if required.

**14** Fold the whole scarf up into a parcel, with the fibres inside, then drop the parcel onto your work surface about 20 times. Unfold, check that the fibres are not felting to themselves, refold and drop it another 20 times.

**15** Repeat this stage until you have the desired final effect and size. You will probably have to drop the scarf 80 or 100 times before this is achieved, but check and refold it after every 20 drops so you can judge how it is progressing. Rinse the scarf thoroughly in cold water, adding a few drops of vinegar to the final rinse, reshape it and dry flat.

# carnival time

**This is a really fun scarf**, with multi-coloured tufts that remind me of all the vibrant colours and passion of Carnival. To be in the Caribbean at Carnival time is to have your senses assaulted by sounds, smells, tastes and sights.

This is a reversible scarf in which two contrasting colours of merino fibres create a sandwich with a layer of red silk chiffon in the middle. The tufts are made from purchased chunky slub wool knitting yarn. Make the scarf in fabulous colours and it will brighten up even the dullest outfit and give it that Caribbean zing!

## tools and materials

towel

2 pieces of bubble wrap, 45 x 170cm (18 x 66 in.)

red silk chiffon, 40 x 165cm (16 x 64 in.)

50g (2 oz) merino fleece in each of fuchsia pink and purple

net, 45 x 170cm (18 x 66 in.)

plastic bottle with holes in lid

olive oil soap

small plastic bag

swimming 'noodle' or similar and ties

cane blind

100g (4 oz) chunky slub wool yarn, cut into 15cm (6 in.) lengths

stiletto, or similar, to make holes in scarf

darning needle

## finished size

30 x 120cm (12 x 48 in.)

# to make the carnival time scarf

**1** Lay a piece of bubble wrap, bubble side down, on the towel. Place a piece of red silk chiffon on top, allowing 30 per cent extra for shrinkage. Lay down an even layer of fuchsia pink merino wool fibres along the silk, with all the fibres lying in the same direction, until the whole of the fabric is covered.

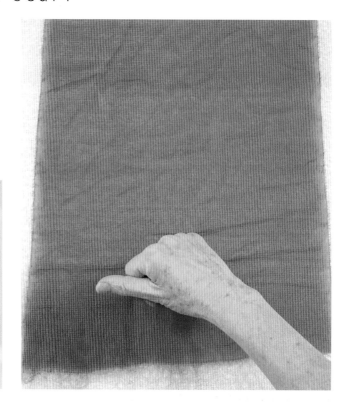

## tip

If you apply a very light spray of water to the silk fabric after you have laid it on the bubble wrap, then smooth the fabric with your hands, you will find that it stays in place better when you are laying the wool fibres on top.

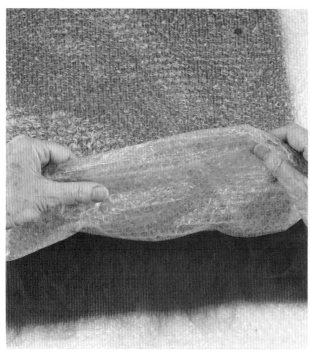

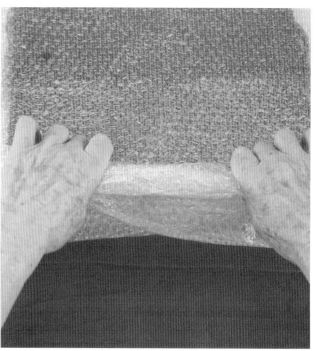

**2** Place a second piece of bubble wrap over the scarf, press down with your hands to compress the fibres, then flip the package over.

**3** Carefully remove the top layer of bubble wrap.

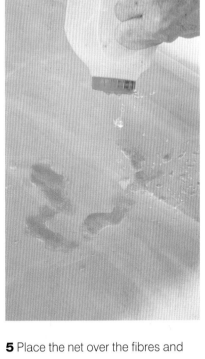

**4** Repeat step 1, this time using purple merino wool fibres. The direction in which you lay the fibres is not important.

**5** Place the net over the fibres and sprinkle with cold water. Press down on the net with the flat of your hand so that the merino fibres absorb the water.

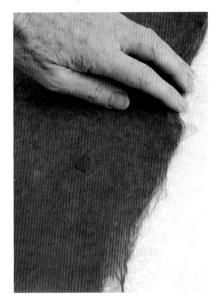

**6** Apply soap gently over the entire surface of the scarf.

**7** With your hand in a plastic bag, rub gently working from one end of the scarf to the other.

**8** When the fibres have adhered to each other, remove the net and tidy the edges of the scarf if necessary.

**9** Place the second sheet of bubble wrap over the scarf, smooth side down and roll it up around a swimming noodle. Tie firmly, roll 100 times, unwrap, straighten, roll up again from the other end and roll another 100 times.

**10** Unwrap, straighten the scarf, then place the scarf directly onto a cane blind. Roll up, tie firmly and roll 50 times. Unwrap, straighten the scarf, roll it up from the other end and roll a further 50 times.

**11** Unwrap and gently reapply soap to the entire scarf. Sprinkle a little more water on at this stage if necessary, as the scarf needs to be quite wet for the next stage.

**12** Fold the scarf into a package, then drop it 25 times onto your work surface. Unfold, reshape, refold and drop again 25 times.

**13** Repeat this stage until the scarf has shrunk by about 25–30 per cent. Rinse the scarf several times in cold water, adding a few drops of vinegar to the final rinse. Pull the scarf into shape, dry flat and press the back with the iron on a wool setting while still slightly damp.

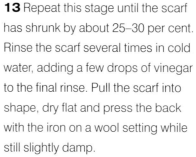

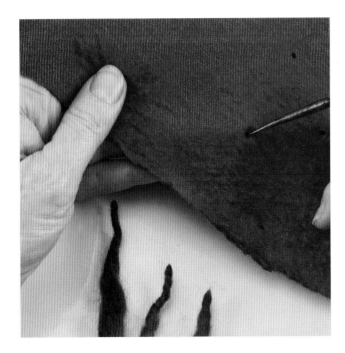

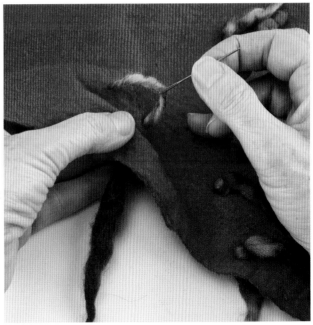

**14** When the scarf is completely dry, lightly mark the points at which you want to place the tufts. Cut the yarn into pieces about 15cm (6 in.) long. Carefully pierce the scarf at each marked point with a stiletto or similar.

**15** Thread a length of cut yarn through a darning needle and pull the yarn through the hole.

**16** With the yarn halfway through the hole, tie a knot close to the scarf on each side to hold the tuft in place. Repeat as necessary for the desired effect.

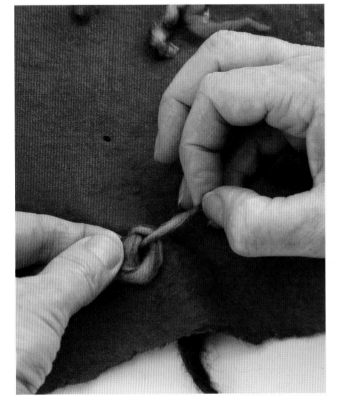

### tip
I only placed tufts at each end to form a kind of fringe, but you could also put them along the whole length of the scarf for a more dramatic effect.

# starfish

**This very delicate scarf** is made entirely from pre-felts similar to those used in the Underwater scarf (page 108). I find the starfish shape particularly enchanting and often use it in my work. I made this scarf as an experiment, just to see how a scarf would turn out using only adjoining motifs. The motifs are felted onto a backing fabric for extra strength and I was really pleased with the scarf that resulted.

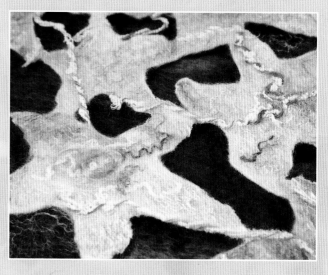

## Method of felting

First, I made a pre-felt about 60cm (24 in.) square by laying down one thin layer of white merino, followed by a second layer of white and pastel colours. (I mixed merino and silk tussah fibres for this layer and then placed random threads, yarns and tiny scraps of fabric on top for extra interest and texture.)

To make the template, I drew a starfish on thin plastic and cut it out. (There is a starfish template on page 125 that you can trace.) I pinned the template to the pre-felts and cut out 30–35 motifs. I placed the motifs on a piece of silk tulle measuring roughly 40 x 175cm (16 x 53 in.) with the starfish points touching wherever possible. I covered the scarf with net, then wetted, soaped, rubbed and rolled it. It was then felted as in steps14 and 15 of the Underwater scarf (page108). While the scarf was still slightly damp, I gently pressed the back with an iron on the wool setting.

# aqua wrap with starfish pin

**This photo shows the fabulous colours** of the Caribbean – brightly painted shacks and buildings, white beaches and water that goes from a soft aqua through turquoise to the marine blue of deeper waters. The shades of the ocean are so beautiful that I just had to make a wrap to remind myself of them. The wrap is simple to make and a little pin in the shape of a starfish adds the finishing touch.

## Method of felting

I laid down two layers of merino wool tops to cover an area 75 x 200cm (30 x 80 in.), with the fibres on the first layer lying lengthwise and the top layer across the width. At each end I used about 20cm (8 in.) of light sand-coloured fleece and, for the main part, I mixed blues and deep greens. Then I added various silks, yarns, embroidery thread and tufts of white and coloured tussah silk to lend texture and touches of colour. I wetted, soaped, rolled and completed the scarf in the usual way. When making a large piece, it's important to check carefully that it is felted in the middle. You may need to roll the piece more than 600 times before this is achieved.

## starfish pin

I made the starfish pin in exactly the same way as the Daisy Brooch on page 32, by making a piece of felt from three layers of white fleece to which I had added a little silk. I cut out the shape using the starfish template on page 125 and machine stitched around the edge of the motif for extra definition, before sewing a brooch pin to the back to complete the piece.

# templates

Enlarge each template by 130% on the photocopier, and then trace around it.

If you are cutting motifs from damp pre–felts, cut templates out of a piece of thin plastic; if you are using dry pre–felts, you can use paper or card.

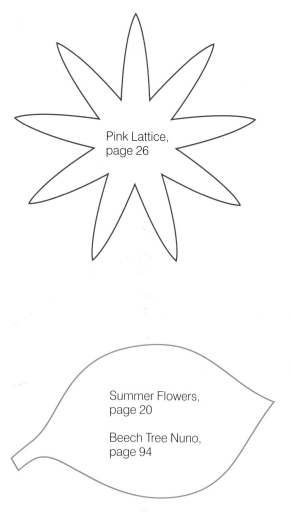

Pink Lattice,
page 26

Summer Flowers,
page 20

Beech Tree Nuno,
page 94

Summer Flowers,
page 20

Daisy Brooch,
page 32

Sycamore,
page 66

Underwater,
page 108

Starfish,
page 120

Starfish Pin,
page 122

Underwater,
page 108

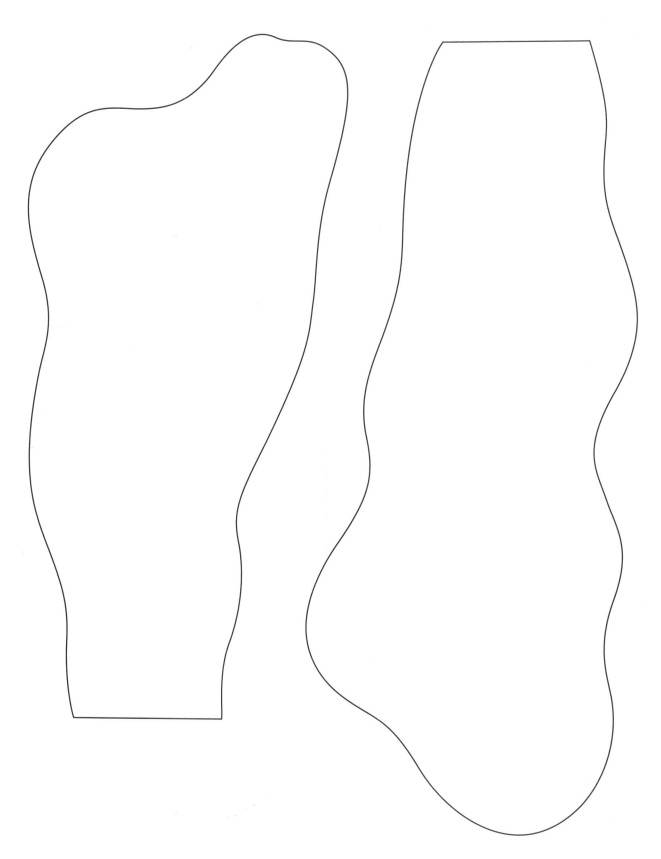

Silly Seaweed,
page 52

# index

This index gives page references
to the projects found in the book.
Page numbers in *italics* refer to the
main illustration.  As many materials
and techniques are used throughout
the book, the page references are
intended to direct the reader to
substantial entries only.

# acknowledgements

I would like to thank all at Breslich & Foss, especially Janet
Ravenscroft for 'finding' me and offering me the chance to
write this book; Lizzie for fab photography and wonderful
hospitality; all my children and my girlfriends for being so
supportive in all sorts of ways, even though they seem to think
I'm just a bit of a hippy… Also Sarah in Antigua for giving me
the opportunity to discover that beautiful paradise island.
Lastly to Kim, for always being such an inspiration and
without whose encouragement I would never be doing what
I'm doing today. Oh, and I nearly forgot Inklie, my very springy
spaniel. Now that the book is finished, she will get two walks
again every day, I promise!

Breslich & Foss Ltd would like to thank the following people
for their help in creating the book:

Editorial assistance **Jane Birch**
Templates **Stephen Dew**
Copy editing **Sarah Hoggett**
Photographs on pages 14–17, 26 and 122 (top)
by **Jill Denton**